Shame and the Church

Shame and the Church

Exploring and Transforming Practice

Sally Nash

scm press

Published in 2020 by SCM Press
Editorial office
3rd Floor, Invicta House,
108–114 Golden Lane,
London ECIY OTG, UK
www.scmpress.co.uk

SCM Press is an imprint of Hymns Ancient & Modern Ltd
(a registered charity)

Hymns Ancient & Modern® is a registered trademark of
Hymns Ancient & Modern Ltd
13A Hellesdon Park Road, Norwich,
Norfolk NR6 5DR, UK

British Library Cataloguing in Publication data

A catalogue record for this book is available
from the British Library

978-0-334-05884-7

Typeset by Manila Typesetting Company
Printed and bound by CPI Group (UK) Ltd

Contents

Acknowledgements

The origins of this book were in the study I undertook as part of my ordination training. I am thankful to the Bishop of Birmingham, David Urquhart, who allowed me to do this and to David Hewlett and Stephen Pattison, who were willing to share their wisdom with me as supervisors. Stephen's own writing and teaching on this subject as well as many conversations have taught me so much. I also shared much of this journey of writing with Helen Blake and have wonderful memories of meals together and hospitality in Birmingham, Sydney, the Blue Mountains and Cornwall.

I am immensely grateful to the many people who shared their experiences with me, both anonymously through my questionnaires and through focus groups and responses to things I had posted on social media. These include several people who wrote things specifically for the book and who are named in the relevant places (if they wanted to be). The book would not have been written without these contributions.

I am appreciative of the help of several people who very kindly commented on a final draft of the book and made it a better one: Helen Blake, Paul Goodliff, David Hewlett, Rachel Hudson, Catherine Matlock and Stephen Pattison. Thanks also to David Shervington, my editor at SCM Press, for his work on my text.

The book is dedicated with gratitude to all those whose experience, wisdom and story is reflected within it.

Preface

I have written this book because of my own experiences over many years, and because I love the church and hate that which damages her. Some of my passion to address shame is encapsulated by Jamieson: 'If false guilt (What you did was wrong!) has caused some to walk away from the church, shaming (You are a bad person!) has done far greater damage' (2016, pp. 57–8). I hope that the book will help to raise awareness of shame in the church and prevent some of the difficult practices that have hurt people and caused them to walk away from a body they had hoped to belong to. I am very grateful to all of the people who shared their stories with me, often through an anonymous online survey. This has helped me understand shame in greater depth and become more aware of the ways in which it is manifested in the church.

How to Use this Book

I am a practical theologian and theological educator as well as a Church of England priest licensed to a parish in Birmingham. Ministry has been both my paid and voluntary work for over 35 years. This dual focus for ministry has been a tension for me as I wrote this book. I want to ensure that anyone who would like to study shame in more depth has plenty of leads to follow through my references but, more importantly, I want the book to be accessible to anyone with an interest in this topic. I recommend reading Chapter 1 first as it introduces all the concepts that are unpacked in the rest of the book. The other chapters can be read in order but all stand alone too and can be read whenever they seem to address what you want to reflect on. Each chapter has questions to aid reflection on its content and these can be explored individually or in a group.

Structure of the book

The book consists of three main parts:

Chapters 1 and 2 present some of my theoretical and theological underpinning, signposting other authors which may be helpful for anyone wanting to study shame in more detail for themselves. Chapter 1 contains my definitions of shame and introduces a typology of shame in the church, which I devised to help raise awareness of shame and our propensity to shame or be shamed.

In Chapter 2, I offer some biblical perspectives on the topic drawn from two specific areas: the creation narratives (where shame is first encountered) and the life and work of Jesus (as our primary exemplar in ministry). The chapter contains quite detailed references for anyone who wants to read around the biblical background material in greater depth.

Chapters 3 to 5 explain the typology that I devised to understand shame in the church and the different ways it is manifested. These chapters in particular are full of people's experiences which help to illustrate the different types of shame. Chapter 3 describes personal shame and Chapter 4 communal shame. The remainder of the typology – relational, structural, theological and historical shame – is discussed in Chapter 5.

Chapters 6 to 8 focus specifically on ministerial practice. Liturgy and ritual are considered in Chapter 6, which includes examples of material that can be used in practice or can act as a starting point to develop your own. Teaching and learning are the focus for Chapter 7. Creating a less shaming church is explored in Chapter 8, which includes a case study on Christmas.

Remembering what is true

What I find most difficult about shame is that it can be so easy to embrace falsehood and to negate who God is and the truth of what God says about us. Graham summarizes this powerfully:

> If shame tells me that I'm defective, grace tells me that I'm valuable. Shame's greatest weapon is the fear of judgment, grace's even greater weapon is the relief of unconditional love. Shame says that because I am flawed I am unacceptable, grace says that though I am flawed I am cherished. Shame believes that the opinion of others is what matters, grace believes that the opinion of God is what matters. Shame is the language of the serpent, grace is the language of Jesus.

> The enemy uses shame to hold us back from true freedom. Shame has a voice – lies! (2009, p. 42)

My hope for this book is that it will raise awareness of shame – of the ways that we are shamed, and the ways we may shame others – with the end goal of liberating people into all that God created them to be.

PART I

Defining Shame

1

Defining Shame and a Typology of Shame in the Church

I just want to do God's will.
And He's allowed me to go up to the mountain.
And I've looked over. And I've seen the Promised Land.
(Martin Luther King's last speech, 1968)

Treasure and a promised land

My promised land after ten years of studying shame in the church is a church that does not have 'disgrace shame' as part of its repertoire for those who have done nothing wrong in the eyes of God. Shame is about who we are, our very being, it is about feeling flawed, defective, unlovable. In over 30 years of Christian ministry I have seen much damage done to individuals, groups and communities who experience shaming at the hands of other Christians, sometimes based on ignorance, fear or difference. When, after 25 years of full-time Christian ministry, God called me to be ordained as a priest in the Church of England, I thought it was important to re-examine ministry in practice. This led me to study shame and the church with a particular focus on what Smedes (1993) refers to as the shame we don't deserve. McNish argues:

> It is ironic but perhaps not surprising that a faith which exalts as part of the Godhead itself a man who spent his life loving and accepting people out of shame, a person who took upon himself the ultimate shame – a man/God who 'endured the cross, disregarding its shame, and has taken his seat at the right hand of the throne of God' (Hebrews

> 12.2) – has emerged as the 'shamingest' institution of all. (2004, p. 188)

While this may be a disputable claim, and is not everyone's experience, I wanted to play my part in trying to change this.

As part of my ordination service the Bishop said: 'Remember always with thanksgiving that the treasure now to be entrusted to you is Christ's own flock, bought by the shedding of his blood on the cross. It is to him that you will render account for your stewardship of his people' (*Common Worship*). If fire engulfed our home, then the thing that I would grab would be my box of treasures. There is little of value to anyone else in that box, but within it are things that I cherish, protect, value and honour in much the same way as I want to do (although don't always succeed) with those for whom God has called me to care. If I treasure someone then why would I want to cause them to suffer the following:

> When you are shamed, the space around you is eviscerated. Now your every move draws negative attention. Hostility and disgust are flung at you. It is impossible from outside to even imagine the humiliation that shame brings. All the natural shelter and support around your presence is taken from you . . . Everything about you is telescoped into the single view of this one shameful thing. Everything else is forgotten. A kind of psychological murdering is done. The mystery of your life is reduced to one thing. You become a 'thing of shame'. (O'Donohue 1998, p. 115)

While this may be a strong experience of shame, it begins to give a glimpse of what it can do to someone, and why I have such a passion that such shaming should be eliminated from pastoral practice. A gentler but also powerful description was written as part of a group I was facilitating:

> I learned the truth at 23
> That church was meant for men, not me

That girls should learn with quiet grace
And never run about the place
I learned that leaders had to be
Clothed in respectability
And women should modestly obey
And know the proper words to pray
And not be excited or too loud
Or speak their mind, 'cause that was proud
And turn up everywhere on time
And always toe the party line . . .
(Practical Theology Seminar participant)

Can you imagine what that does to you day after day, week after week, not being able to be who God created you to be because the expectations of you were so oppressive? It is difficult not to feel shame when we are not what others (whose opinions we value) want us to be. At its extreme this can be our experience:

> For some of us, shame does not come and go. For some of us, shame is a constant emotional state. It is a cloud that follows us everywhere. This cloud can become a belief that at the base of our identity we are poison. We come to believe that there is something wrong in us that we cannot fix, and we are afraid that others will find out. This belief is a lie. (McMillan 2006, p. 158)

This is why it is important to identify and process people's shame and why trying to avoid people getting to this place is important. As human beings, the base of our identity is that we are made in the image of God; we cannot be poison if this is so.

Shame is a concept that has come to the fore recently in both popular culture and the church. For example, Brené Brown's (2012) TED (Technology, Entertainment and Design) talk has done much to bring the topic to wider attention along with her helpful books. Cultural commentator Jon Ronson's book *So you've been publicly shamed* (2015) surveys shaming in media, including social media and other contexts. And *Christianity*

Today proclaimed the return of shame in a cover story in 2015 (Crouch 2015). While this is the broader context of this book, shame is still a bit of a slippery concept which can be hard to define, identify and respond to. The purpose of this book is to present a typology of shame in the church involving six different dimensions in the hope that it will help identify ways in which shaming might occur and to make some suggestions about how ministerial practice can be less shaming.

My experiences of shame

One of my personal principles for ministry is that I will not ask anyone to do something I am unwilling to do myself. Therefore, before I asked others to tell me their stories of shame, I had to look at my own. What I discovered was that it was an early experience at school that triggered my interest in shame and left me with an underlying distrust of institutions. I have tried to get into the mind of my eight-year-old self when presented with a maths exercise to find out the average weight of the class:

> I have that horrible knotted feeling in my stomach. Why would they ask that question? That's so horrible, so mean, I don't want to be at school. As the teacher begins to go around the class, I put my hand up – 'I feel ill, can I go and sit quietly for a bit please?' The feeling of relief when I am sent to the nurse but the feeling of dread at having to repeat the lies. The last thing in the world I want to do is say how much I weigh, I know I am a bit chubby but I am tall and sporty too, but no one will take any notice of that. They will just laugh as they see I weigh more than most of the boys. I don't believe it, they are still doing the exercise and I thought I had avoided it. I chose a low figure and ignored the looks of unbelief but I blushed, felt bad about myself and wondered why school wanted to show me up like that.

That is my first clear memory of shame, although there obviously would have been others. I can still feel the shame half a century on, although only as an adult could I put a name to what it was I felt. I reconnect with the memory each time the doctor wants me to get on the scales – sometimes for issues that cannot possibly be related to my weight. This used to put me off going to my doctor – and I know how foolish that is, but shame causes me to withdraw and hide. There was a part of me that did not want to open myself up to another lecture that would make me feel like a shamed child again. One of the totally unexpected by-products of doing this research was that it has somehow liberated me to lose weight and sustain most of that weight loss for longer than I ever have before (Nash 2016).

I know these are not church-related stories. I do not have any childhood memories of being shamed at church, perhaps in part because I was largely a quiet, compliant child who enjoyed Sunday School and going to church. I include them to show how shame can be triggered in many different ways and how even a single instance of it can have a long-term influence on our lives. However, as I got older shame and church began to come together. Cultural expectations and judgements meant there was sometimes a lingering shame over who I was and, perhaps more, who I was not, as well as a growing disquiet over the way a theology of women in ministry was modelled. In my teenage and young adult experience, there were many things said that did not resonate with the loving God that I knew from my childhood. This has always left me feeling a slight dissonance between my faith and what others proclaimed, and often I thought these others knew better than me. On more than one occasion I have experienced vicarious shame on behalf of those who were the focus of unloving words or actions as well as feeling shame because I may have done this too, believing I was doing what God wanted.

I am a childless (not by choice) married woman, a barren woman to use the biblical language. I have felt shame over this, particularly when reading the Bible in an uncritical way where barrenness is seen as a punishment by God. Reading of how God answered the prayer of some is also painful and always raises the question why did God not answer our prayers? I detest being asked if I have a family because I never know quite how to reply, and sometimes – and perhaps I am being over-sensitive – pick up a hint that I am obviously not a real woman if I do not have children or cannot possibly be fulfilled without them. Thus, elements of shame linger and can be evoked quite unexpectedly.

The older and more experienced in ministry I have become, the more complex and grey things seem with few right answers and many choices that need wisdom and love. Most of the time now I am content with who God has created me to be and much less often look at others and desire to be like them. It has taken many years to get to this point and understanding shame has helped get to this place. Comparing myself to others and thinking I fall short is a classic sign of shame. I now recognize much more quickly contexts where I may respond with shame and can often mitigate that or at least diminish the impact of the initial trigger and response.

What is shame?

Once we are aware of shame, we encounter it everywhere: 'it is ubiquitous, seeping into every nook and cranny of life. It is pernicious, infesting not just our thoughts, but our sensations, images, feelings and, of course, ultimately, our behaviour. It just doesn't seem to go away' (Thompson 2015, p. 10). There is no one agreed way of defining shame and there is some confusion as to the difference between shame and guilt. There is broad agreement that guilt tends to focus on what we have done and is other-focused, but shame is about who we are and impacts our sense of self. Thus, we address guilt often by changing our behaviour, whereas with shame we need to change the way we think about ourselves, which isn't always easy.

Looking at dictionary definitions of shame suggests that the word may be derived from a pre-Germanic word, *skem*, which means covering ourselves. This has echoes of the story in Genesis 3 where Adam and Eve were made clothes by God to cover the shame they experienced when they realized they were naked. A thesaurus offers a range of synonyms for the noun shame:

contempt, degradation, derision, discomposure, discredit, disesteem, dishonour, disrepute, guilt, humiliation, ignominy, ill repute, infamy, loss of face, mortification, odium, opprobrium, reproach, scandal, self-disgust, self-reproach, self-reproof, shamefacedness, skeleton in the cupboard, smear, stigma. The synonyms for the verb shame are: cut down to size, debase, defile, degrade, discredit, dishonour, give a black eye, humble, humiliate, mortify, reproach, ridicule, smear, stain. Both the lists contain words that relate to experiences most people would want to avoid and that can be very difficult to move on from. One of the complications is that in English, unlike most European languages, there are not different words for disgrace and discretion shame.

This book is largely about disgrace shame as that is what can damage or destroy people's lives while discretion or healthy shame is what enables a society to function with some boundaries. Thus, there are clear cultural expectations about such things as clothing, appropriate touch and modes of behaviour, which means we usually know what to do to fit in. This also explains why sometimes we feel uncomfortable, or shamed, when we have (usually inadvertently) broken these cultural norms. Disgrace shame tends to happen after we have acted and discretion shame before we act. Discretion shame is also important in relation to protection against exposure, protecting the private dimension of human activity, tact, respecting others, making appropriate choices and exercising restraint. Thus, shame is not necessarily all bad for us.

I am mainly using the term 'experiencing' in relation to shame, rather than 'feeling', as I want to get away from thinking of shame solely as an emotion. Within a Western context emotion is often contrasted unhelpfully with reason, and discussions about shame should not be easily dismissed by those who mistrust emotion. However, I am certainly not denying that we feel shame and that these feelings can be very powerful or that shame can impact the way that we express other emotions. Shame has a range of different elements and is something that is quite hard to define. These include being both healthy and unhealthy, the opposite of pride and what distinguishes humanity from other creatures. Shame can be felt anywhere, over anything, and can change over time and culture. There is always an audience for shame, even if it is an idealized self. Shame is something which can be both felt individually and experienced as a social sanction. It has physiological, cognitive and behavioural consequences on us that impact our ability to think clearly, talk and act; it is often associated with blushing, turning away or hiding our face. Shame is also masked behind anger, contempt, depression, superiority or denial. Guilt and shame are often distinguished by saying that guilt is about our actions whereas shame encompasses who we are, the whole self. Appendix 1 has this in list form with references to show where my thinking has come from.

Healthy shame

In this first chapter I want to make it clear that I believe that shame can be healthy and is an integral part of being human. Shame helps us realize when there is something wrong that we may want to address or amend; it makes a functioning society and relationships possible. Bradshaw (2005) offers a helpful summary of what healthy shame looks like: it provides a natural boundary and gives us permission to be human and develop identity and intimacy, to maintain a sense of dignity bringing a sense of awe, reverence and modesty. It can also assist us in avoiding unhelpful blaming of self or others and can lead to a critically examined conscience.

Causes of shame

It is not possible to list all the causes of shame but identifying some of them can help both self and pastoral awareness. These triggers for shame can be both personal and structural. The latter can include the use of stereotypes, all sorts of 'isms' such as sexism or racism and other forms of oppression. Individually shame can be the result of insensitivity, unhelpful coping mechanisms (e.g. self-harm, drugs, eating disorders), ridicule, banter, social media comments, comparison, self-blame, feeling dependent, rejection, for example. Some individuals may be more shame-prone than others. Smedes (1993) suggests that those who may be in this category include what he calls guilt-spreaders; the overly responsible; obsessive moralizers; compulsive comparers; approval addicts; never deserving; those condemned by bad memories or their dreams; and those dwelling in the shadow a of parent or family member. Nathanson identifies eight causes of shame: matters of personal size, strength, ability, skill (I am weak or stupid); dependence/independence (helplessness); competition (I am a loser); sense of self (I am defective); personal attractiveness (I am ugly or deformed); sexuality (something wrong with me sexually); issues of seeing and being seen (wanting to escape from exposure); wishes and fears about closeness (feeling unlovable and wanting to be left alone) (1992, p. 317). Wurmser (1997) identifies six main areas that can cause shame, which are based around our self-perception as being weak; dirty, messy or disgusting; defective physically or mentally; lacking control over body functions and or feelings; inappropriate or dangerous sexual excitement or activity. Broadly, McNish suggests that

> shame arises out of life in the body and it often has reference, directly or indirectly, to the needs, desires, situation, limitations or condition of the body. It arises out of the uniquely human experience of being a creature, yet feeling somehow that one is spirit, and of God as well. One is helpless and powerless in so many ways, and it is experienced as humiliating. (2003, p. 7)

Shame originates in early childhood experiences and is often related to our sense of helplessness. It is clearly present at the toddler stage. It can begin to emerge at the time we are totally dependent on parents or carers for love and when these relationships go wrong, shame may be the response (cf. Erikson 1995). Attachment theory also suggests that a child who feels unwanted by their parents can end up feeling unwantable by anyone and this is also a characteristic of shame (Bowlby 1973). Often when we blush, that is shame having a physical manifestation (Probyn

2005). Thus, shame can be triggered by a very wide range of issues, activities or experiences and may have deep roots. What is important is recognizing what is being experienced as shame and then seeking to help ourselves or others work through it.

Consequences of shame

Shame has consequences in people's lives. Positively, shame can

- act as a reminder to behave in a particular way in context; this is often cultural too and churches may have very clear practices here (not always positive);
- help maintain privacy and boundaries in relationships; for example, many of us have had 'too much information' shared with us or not known how to respond to what seems like an over-personal question;
- offer moral motivation to act appropriately, even when there is no-one watching us or may never be found out.

Negatively, on the other hand, it brings with it

- negative feelings such as feeling paralysed, helpless, passive; unlovable and worthless; exposed; flawed, defective and inferior; weak, inadequate, a loser, dirty, infantile; and fear of abandonment; woundedness;
- negative self-perceptions such as feeling small and shrinking; painfully diminished; defective and unworthy; sense of self-respect doubted; cloud that follows us, feeling at heart of identity we are poison; inferiority complex; seeping sense of badness; threat to integrity; fundamentally deficient as a human; contempt for self; loss of face, fall from grace, being unfixable; threat to sense one can be at peace in the world;
- physiological or physical reactions such as a desire to hide, crawl away or die; feeling of being watched; potentially experiencing tears, rage or blushing; undischarged hostility including feeling rage towards someone then turning it back on oneself; getting trapped in a shame–rage–revenge cycle.

All of these negative consequences can be immensely powerful in our lives and can inhibit us from living life to the full, particularly when they are deep-seated and long-standing and we do not have the support to help us move beyond them. One of the reasons I want to raise awareness of shame is that it can mar the image of God in us and our capacity to pursue our vocation to become fully the person God created us to be.

Drawing a definition together

A phenomenological definition seeks to describe something in detail. Because of the multifaceted nature of shame, I found that developing a phenomenological definition enabled me to draw on my reading, research and experience:

> Shame may be either constraining or estranging having either a beneficial or negative consequence; is contextually determined in relation to a real or imaginary audience and can arise from a sense of exposure and vulnerability which impacts the whole of self; may include a loss of status, identity and belonging; produces feelings of unworthiness, powerlessness, self-contempt, incongruence; results in seeing self as flawed, unlovable, deficient, contaminated, dirty; acts as a threat to trust; often causes significant suffering to self and sometimes others; acts as an incentive to maintaining healthy boundaries, relationships and concern for others; may be manifest in many ways including physiological, a desire to withdraw or hide, or spark a shame/rage cycle.

Shame in institutions

While we may most often think about shame as personal, there is also a clear communal dimension to it. Anthropologist Mary Douglas' book *How Institutions Think* (1987) suggests that institutions influence the way that we think, and that this can include the way we experience shame. Shame has been seen communally in a variety of ways which can involve loss of status, place or identity. One example is having a national character with shame, rage and revenge cycles which have the potential for war or conflict. Nazi Germany is an example of this. Another dimension is how some groups can be seen as polluting and acting as a threat to the social bond with a consequential impact on community cohesion; attitudes to travellers or refugees are examples of this. Also, people in an organization may feel collective shame in response to something that happens or they can psychologically distance themselves from identifying with an organization because of the shame they feel in relation to leaders, for example.

Shame in institutions may be seen as structural sin which 'describes the embodiment of sin in structures which in turn produce further disvalues in the form of intolerance, inequality and all manners of injustice' (Connolly 2002, p. 112). In using this term, I am suggesting that sometimes sinful attitudes, words, actions and so on may be incorporated into the practices and structures of institutions to the detriment of particular individuals or groups.

Evidence from other sectors suggests that shame in relation to institutions may be helpful for thinking about how and where it may occur in the church. Davidoff argues that shame 'is a powerful force in slowing or preventing improvement [and] unless or until shame is confronted and dealt with, progress in improvement will be slow' (2002, p. 1). He writes this in relation to doctors admitting to patients that they have done something wrong. For clergy this may perhaps be even more complex as in some traditions the notion that God has done something wrong may be implicit in an admission. Research in the area of social marketing suggests that using shame is ineffective as an approach to get people to do the right thing; people talked about such issues as hopelessness and depression in response to such shaming approaches (Brennan and Binney 2010). The implications of using shaming in the church may be the same for some people.

Writing more specifically about the church, McNish (2004) suggests that in a distorted form shame can destroy communities and may foster toxic shame. Pattison (2000) suggests that the church needs to recognize the way some of her ideas and practices can exacerbate or even create shame in people. In some traditions, the way that priesthood and religious life was raised 'to a position of sanctity that was beyond recrimination [which] facilitated a tendency to protect perpetrators and blame (and shame) victims' (Clough 2010, p. 30) means that the church can be a shaming institution. This is particularly true of some of the responses to sexual abuse, historical cover-ups and an unwillingness to acknowledge that there are some who have abused the trust of their role and caused significant long-term damage to people. The case of the Anglican Bishop Peter Ball and those who colluded, covered up and dealt badly with victims is a clear example of this. To try to encapsulate some of the reflections on shame in an institutional context I developed a working definition of institutional shame:

> the consequence of practices, structures, processes, behaviour, attitudes and liturgy that people encounter through their involvement in and with the church and other Christian institutions, which fail to reflect the reality of the body of Christ as exemplifying the love, life, work and example of Jesus and which engender shame in individuals, groups or communities.

I am not suggesting that shaming is always intentional, manipulative or malicious. What I am saying is that much of it may be inadvertent or careless and the perpetrator unaware of the consequences unless they are alerted to the consequence of their actions.

Introducing the typology of shame in the church

The idea to develop a typology of shame emerged out of an attempt to define shame in the church and realizing that it was often hidden, misinterpreted as something else and difficult to talk about with people. A typology is a classification of something with common characteristics which helps explain the different ways something may be experienced. My typology has six domains, different areas in which shame may be experienced in a church setting:

- ***Personal shame*** relates to shame experienced by an individual as a consequence of his or her relationship with the church.
- ***Communal shame*** relates to shame which is experienced at a group or congregational level.
- ***Relational shame*** is experienced as a consequence of identification with people who commit shameful acts within the church, particularly, but not exclusively, leaders.
- ***Structural shame*** relates to shame that is a consequence of what the church or organization says, does, or believes at an institutional level.
- ***Theological shame*** is experienced when people's view of God or their core beliefs are challenged, opposed, ridiculed or misrepresented.
- ***Historical shame*** relates to something that has happened in the church in the past that is often not spoken about but still has an impact on current church life.

Within each of these six areas I then identified core words and concepts emerging from my research and personal and ministerial experience that helped to explain that element of shame. The words also offer an alternative vocabulary for both identifying and discussing shame. They are summarized in Table 1. The bracketed element of the word illustrates that both uses of the word may trigger shame. Thus, I can experience shame through complying with something that deep within I feel is wrong – in doing this I am contravening my personal principles. Or I can feel shame because of non-compliance which although satisfying my own convictions, means that I feel shame about not being a 'good' church member because I don't toe the party line. Being made to feel insufficient is another area and being childless often triggers such a feeling. Feeling like a nonentity in a context can also cause shame. With communal shame there are issues around being stigmatized, disaffected and disempowered, which can relate to particular groups or categories in the church. Vicarious shame is that which we feel on behalf of another. We can also feel shame when we collude with what the structures proclaim as right but also when we do not as it may feel like we have let the side down. Fragmenting can occur when we split over something, not always a deep theological issue, and ultimately for some a lack of unity causes shame. Theological shame can occur through both association and disassociation when we do or do not agree with a particular theological stance; the ordination of women, for example, is one area where this has been prevalent. Dissonance occurs when there is a gap between what is proclaimed and what happens in reality. Buried and residual elements of shame are often areas that affect the life of a church: there is a sense that something is wrong, but if no-one speaks about them they can cause confusion as to what is really happening.

Domain	*Facets of shame*
Personal	(Non)complying (Non)conforming Insufficiency Nonentity
Communal	Stigmatizing Disaffecting Disempowering
Relational	Vicarious
Structural	(Un)colluding Fragmenting
Theological	Associative Dissociative Dissonant
Historical	Buried Residual

Table 1. Typology of shame in the church.

The typology was also used as a framework for some empirical research. In total 312 people accessed anonymous questionnaires using an online survey. They consisted of 110 church leaders, 109 church members and 43 theological educators (the latter were my professional context) and a further 50 people who completed the survey at a later date. Eleven people attended a focus group and reflected the make-up of those who had completed the survey. The rest of the book draws on this research as well as some subsequent surveys and interactions with those who contacted me when I posted on social media about my research. Quotations from the research and this communication are in italics so that the voice of those who shared their stories can be heard authentically. See Appendix 2 for a summary of themes from the research.

Practical theology and ministerial praxis

This book is a piece of practical theology which I understand as 'critical, theological, reflection on the practices of the Church as they interact with the practices of the world, with a view to ensuring and enabling faithful participation in God's redemptive practices in, to and for the world' (Swinton and Mowat 2006, p. 6). This is what I was trying to do in relation to my own ministerial praxis, but I also wanted to encourage others to reflect on their own praxis too. I have chosen to use the word 'praxis' rather than 'practice' in this book. Praxis is more purposeful, implying a thought-through approach that is critical, dynamic and reflective. I have been influenced by Freire's (1966) concept of conscientization and my intention in writing this book is to raise awareness of the way that shame in the church may be triggered or manifested in the hope that I and others may engage in more faithful practice in the light of a gracious and loving God. I hope the book helps congregations become more explicitly aware of shame and how they can support those who are experiencing shame, as well as becoming less shaming.

Conclusion

In this chapter I have sought to explain why I think shame is important through sharing some of my own story; introduce the concept of shame, some of its consequences and its links to institutions and give a brief overview of my typology. This is the theoretical framework that underpins the book. The next chapter introduces the biblical and theological underpinning.

Reflection questions

- Can you recollect a shaming experience from your childhood? If so, can you identify ways in which it impacts you now?
- Do you recognize any of the elements of the typology of shame in the church in your context?
- Are there any words in the facets of shame list in the typology that resonate? What experiences do they evoke?
- What one issue about shame in the church most concerns you?
- What are the current issues that you think are causing shame in the church more widely? How do they impact the local church?

2

Biblical Perspectives on Shame

Introduction

I try to live my life according to biblical guidelines, and when I do not I might feel shame, that I am a bad person. I might also feel guilt, that I have done something wrong, but that is not the focus of this book. I am not going to define 'biblical guidelines' – that would be a book in itself – but a simple example is that I try to demonstrate the fruit of the Spirit as described in Galatians 5.22. I sometimes struggle to be patient in places like the checkout queue, and if I have snapped at the person serving me I then feel shame at not living up to my ideal. I was discipled into a faith that encouraged me to take up my cross, follow Jesus and to seek to become conformed to his image. I understand this to be a life-long task which is both challenging and fulfilling. While studying shame I have become more concerned about the way that the Bible may be interpreted and used both by those experiencing shame and those who are doing the shaming (sometimes inadvertently). This can occur in all theological traditions but usually over different issues.

Exegesis is the critical interpretation of the text and this can be done from a range of perspectives with different commentators not necessarily sharing the same interpretation. I have chosen to begin with Thiselton's 'two horizons' (1980, p. xix) metaphor which involves taking seriously both the horizon of the interpreter and that of the biblical text. In the last chapter, I told some of my own story which gives an insight into where I start from in looking at texts on shame, but we need to be aware that where we are situated in time, history and culture, for example, influences our interpretation as well as our understanding of the culture in which the text was originally written. Shame is very much a cultural concept and the differences in culture between then and now are significant. Within practical theology there is a tension between what is prioritized, whether that should be our experience or the Bible (see Ward 2017 for a discussion of this issue). I tend to be drawn to a Christocentric approach to interpretation which 'should enhance our love of God and neighbour and contribute to human flourishing in terms of justice, mercy and faithfulness' (Pietersen 2011, p. 70). I have also explored feminist perspectives and am often reminded of a poster I saw once which quoted Maya Angelou: 'I am a feminist. I've been female for a long time now. It'd be stupid not to be on my own side.'

This chapter will focus on two parts of the Bible which have particular significance for shame in the church and the praxis of ministry: the creation narratives and the Gospel stories of Jesus. The creation narratives are important as this is where shame is first encountered. The Gospel stories help us to explore the ministry of Jesus in relation to ministerial praxis and shame. I begin each section with an introduction to the broader context which is relevant in the light of studying shame. In beginning this process I was intrigued by Collicutt's suggestion, as a psychologist, that 'if the text is to be received as transformative, a good reading is likely to be dissonant, challenging or ugly' (2012, p. 1). This helped me to be open to fresh perspectives and a range of interpretations beyond those I was familiar with.

Introduction to the Old Testament context

Shame and honour are related concepts which are seen by many scholars as a significant lens for Old Testament study (deSilva 2011). However, there are a breadth of views as to how they may be used as an interpretive lens. At their simplest, honour and shame involve our self-perception, that of others, and our perceived societal value. More fully, honour is 'associated with greatness, dignity, splendour and esteem, as created by the actions of the individual, or his or her family'. Correspondingly, experiencing shame means losing 'virtue, esteem, prestige, courage' (Rabichev 1996, p. 57). Although I am focusing on shame it is important to note the association with honour as this is significant for interpretation and helpful in our praxis.

Within the Old Testament there are at least ten different words with nearly 300 occurrences that reflect various facets of shame (Tennent 2007, p. 83). The most commonly used are *bôš*, a verb meaning to be ashamed; *hārap*, translated as to reproach, dishonour or taunt; and a range of nouns (*bōšet*, *qualôn*, *kĕlimmâ*, *nĕbālâ*, *herpâ*) translated by such words as shame, disgrace, dishonour, insult (Yee 2003, p. 42). However, careful attention needs to be given to the Hebrew words and the associated translations suggesting that 'failure, disappointment, frustration, humiliation and the suffering of harm, can all cause shame within a specific cultural context, yet they are not identical' (Avrahami 2010, p. 302) but this does begin to show the range of potential shame triggers.

Versions of the Bible also translate the original Hebrew using different words. For example, in Psalm 31.17 the word *bôš* is translated or interpreted as 'shame' in the New Revised Standard Version (my default option), 'disgraced' in the New Century Version, 'ashamed' in the King James Version and 'embarrass' in The Message. This illustrates the dilemma of focusing on a term where there is a plurality of words used in a different language and the challenge of understanding their use in the original context. It is also possible that translators' perspectives vary, as shame can be, for example, anthropological (part of a value system), psychological (as an emotion), or theological (in relation to guilt) (Avrahami 2010, p. 307). The concept of shame that is implicit in the translator's understanding may determine the word chosen. From the perspective of the horizon of the text it is important not to read current cultural constructs into a concept; the case of barrenness and infertility is an example of this. Thus, in the Old Testament a main function of having children was economic whereas in contemporary Western society it is emotional (Koepf-Taylor 2013, p. 63). Summarizing an understanding of shaming in the Old Testament, Bechtel (1994) argues that it functioned primarily as:

- a means of controlling behaviour;
- a way of dominating others and thus manipulating social status;
- an approach to maintaining social cohesion through excluding deviants.

Genesis and the creation narratives

'Genesis' is a transliteration of the Greek word for origins; the Hebrew title is *bĕrē'šît* which is normally translated 'in the beginning'. There are various perspectives on this first book of the Bible with little agreement as to the authorship and history. The creation narratives can be seen as a theological account designed to explain to the Israelites their origins and the nature of their God, who was different to other deities in the region. That there are two different stories is explained as Genesis 1.1–2.4a being the creation story and 2.4b–25, an origins story (Rogerson 1991).

At the end of the sixth day God looked at creation and declared that it was very good (Genesis 1.31). Along with being made in the image of God (Genesis 1.27, often described by the term *imago Dei*), this is the source of the value and dignity of humanity. Shame is first mentioned in Genesis 2.25 when Adam and Eve are described as being naked and without shame. Yet after they have eaten fruit from the forbidden tree of the knowledge of good and evil, they seek to hide from God because of the shame of their nakedness. Adam and Eve hid because they realized they had done something wrong; they were guilty. They could have put that right by responding to God's call and restoring the relationship through confession and forgiveness. Instead they hid and experienced shame as a consequence of not facing their guilt. The story helps us to see that sometimes guilt and shame are interlinked but the distinction remains between guilt being about what we have done and shame about who we are.

While there were clearly consequences of their actions, God acts with compassion and makes them clothes to cover their nakedness (Genesis 3.21). God neither leaves them to do that themselves nor insists that they remain naked. This can be seen as a positive action showing God's forgiveness and mercy and sensitivity to their shame. More controversially, some understand God as bestowing honour on them through clothing them because of the way that clothing is a symbol of honour and investiture in the Bible (Wilder 2006). Some commentators, particularly feminists, suggest that it was not necessarily wrong for Eve to pursue wisdom through eating the fruit (McNish 2003) and that it was part of the maturation process preparing them for the world outside of Eden (Bechtel 1993).

The writings of Irenaeus, a second-century theologian and Bishop of Lyons, lend support to these more contemporary accounts of understanding Adam and Eve as growing and maturing, having been given the capacity to choose, using the term 'infantile' (2015, p. 344) to describe humanity. Traditionally, the term 'fall' has been used to describe the story of Adam and Eve eating from the tree of the knowledge of good and evil and being expelled from the garden yet Irenaeus describes this incident as revealing God as 'patient, benign, merciful, mighty to save' (2015, p. 230). The term 'fall' is not used in Genesis 3 and its use in theology is seen as drawing more from the writing of the apostle Paul and Augustine (Arnold 2008, p. 62). Moreover, Genesis 3 is not generally used in the rest of the Old Testament or Jewish literature as an explanation of humanity's fall. Paul in Romans 5.12–21 uses later theological development rather than what the Genesis text specifically says to explain his understanding of the fall (Pietersen 2011, pp. 88–9). No Hebrew word for sin is used until Genesis 4 (Meyers 1993, p. 127) and Alison (1998) notes how his thinking was transformed by the observation that original sin is not part of Jewish doctrine at all. This supports an interpretation of the creation narratives offered here which focuses more on humanity individuating and maturing.

Perhaps a more useful way of interpreting Genesis 3 and 4 in relation to shame is to understand – based on Genesis 4.7: 'If you do well, will you not be accepted? And if you do not do well, sin is lurking at the door; its desire is for you, but you must master it' – that rather than being an integral part of creation 'sin is regarded as an external power which seeks to grip humanity but can be overcome . . . in powerful, mythic form the whole drama of God's good creation, humanity's propensity to spoil that creation and God's gracious provision is laid out' (Pietersen 2011, p. 94). Pietersen thus suggests that the chaos that was present at the beginning of creation in the formless void sometimes breaks in to our lives, rather than seeing sin and violence as part of the structure of creation. This approach can be seen as connecting to the principalities and powers that the authors of some of the New Testament epistles write about (Ephesians 6.12). This leads to identifying a hermeneutic that understands Genesis 3 as the playing out of a 'mythic drama' which raises the issue as to whether humanity will obey their calling to rely on God or seek to try and obtain God's power for themselves – see Philippians 2.5–11 (Pietersen 2011, p. 207). This discussion attempts to take seriously both the first and second horizon but is not the interpretation I have lived with for most of my life. Thus, in my experience this story has been used to exclude and diminish the role of women through a theological perspective that sees women as representative of what humanity needs saving from, nature and flesh (Isherwood 2004, pp. 141–2).

It is perhaps also significant to note that, for some, the creation narratives can be interpreted as seeing God in a negative light and as a starting point for some (from my perspective) distorted perceptions that can make engagement with God difficult:

> The story [Adam and Eve] has been billed as about the 'fall' from innocence. Yet on the surface it has little to do with

innocence. Rather, it is about being driven out of an idyllic place by a disapproving God who does not like being challenged and who defeats the upstarts, a story expressing Oedipal defeat and shame. In the story of the Garden of Eden, disobedience and challenges to God's authority are punished and the authority of God the father reigns supreme. (Kilborne 2002, p. 86)

Such critiques are unhelpful in reinforcing a negative, authoritarian image of God which may exacerbate shame.

Reflection on the creation narratives

In reflecting on the creation narratives in relation to shame in the church and ministerial praxis there are several concepts which might inform our understanding:

- free will distinguishes us from the rest of creation;
- hiding, a flight response, is a common human reaction to conflict;
- the impact of exclusion on identity and relationships;
- a longing in humanity to be at peace with God while feeling inadequate in many ways;
- boundaries and constraints on human behaviour help us to live together and experience the shalom that is possible for God's people;
- a tendency to blame others rather than take responsibility;
- the stories can mediate a view of God that is challenging.

Finally, while I am not looking at the remainder of the Old Testament there is a pattern of God redeeming shame and honouring those who cry to God for help that we find in stories such as those of Moses, Ruth, Hannah, David, Daniel, Nehemiah and Esther (Borges 2013). The Psalms are also full of shame and honour language and reading; for example, Psalm 44 offers insight into the experience of shame and Psalm 62 stresses how honour comes from God. Thus, while I have focused on the creation narratives in this chapter, there are plenty of other places in the Old Testament where we can gain further insights into shame.

Introduction to the New Testament context

As with the Old Testament, shame and honour are related concepts. In New Testament times your honour status was a significant influence on your life, impacting daily living including behaviour, relationships, dress, food, marriage, death rituals, responsibilities, rights and gestures (Neyrey 1998). deSilva describes how honour was understood for New Testament Christians:

> Becoming a disciple of Jesus brings with it adoption into God's family and a share in Christ's honor (John 1.12–13; Rom. 8.14–17; Heb. 2.10; 3.1–6, 14; 1 Pet. 1.23). In this regard God ascribes the honor of God's own household to the believers. The exaltation of Jesus to the highest honor in the cosmos (Eph. 1.20–22) is thus an honor in which all faithful believers now share (Eph. 2.6). This honor, though possessed by the Christian, is yet fully to be enjoyed and yet to be manifested to the world. It remains their inheritance (1 Pet. 1.4). (2000, pp. 73–4)

Honour was both ascribed through the family and acquired through public acknowledgement of achievement. Both honour and the related concept of shame were collective rather than individualistic concepts and the inclusion and exclusion associated with them were significant (Malina 2010). Related to this, conscience is also communal rather than individualistic and public shaming comes through community accusation rather than an internal voice as we more usually experience today (Rohrbaugh 2010) yet it is still experienced by the individual. However, it is important to realize that the New Testament was written in a range of different contexts from the original Gospel settings to some of the more urban environments of the epistles; thus there is not a single New Testament context to understand shame and honour (Osiek 2008). It is helpful to be aware of some of the broad comparisons between shame and honour in contemporary Western societies and in the New Testament:

- honour and shame are internalized and introspective experiences, and can serve as motives to action *versus* honour and shame are externalized social experiences;
- shame is the rejection of an individual's personhood *versus* shame is the rejection of an individual's and group's claims to honour;
- shame provokes feelings of unworthiness in the individual *versus* shame provokes plans of retaliation and vengeance in the group;
- honour is an internalized feeling of social success *versus* honour is an externalized expression of social success. (Malina 2011, p. 156)

However, it is important to remember that honour/shame is significant in majority-world cultures and increased immigration and the significance of global Christianity means that honour and shame are important missiological issues (Georges and Baker 2016).

Purity

Purity is a significant concept in relation to shame as it illuminates some of the Gospel stories. The Pharisees were concerned about the purity of the physical and social body with a focus on external pollution such as unwashed hands (e.g. Mark 7.23) and importing practices from other cultures. However, Jesus takes a different perspective on purity, seeing it as coming out of the social and physical body, whereas sin comes out of the heart. These things violate God's commandments and have the potential to harm the social body. Thus, Jesus' approach could be seen as re-establishing the purity system originally intended by God. One of the important things to note about purity-related sins is their potential to cause shame because of the 'fly in the soup' situation which means that rehabilitation is difficult (Beck 2011, p. 49).

Jesus' encounters with people

The encounters that Jesus has in the Gospels offers us some examples of how the church might engage with those experiencing shame. For example, the ministry of Jesus is often focused on those on the margins of society and 'much of his healing activity appears to question boundaries and taboos, theologies of taint and forms of social exclusion. Invariably, the healings question the social forces that divide society between the pure and contagious, between the righteous and the sinner' (Percy 2012, p. 74). Within the stories of healing encounters between Jesus and individuals there is a theme of restoration of the individual to the community – often involving some change on behalf of the community in order to embrace the poor, the socially outcast or the previously excluded person (Savage 2007) as well as Jesus sometimes asking the individual to change. Savage argues:

> Across the range of Jesus' interactions, we see him on the warpath against all that degrades human dignity and spiritual value. With flexibility and insight he takes the initiative against the social structures, deceptions, defences, learned helplessness, negative thoughts and patterns and paralysing fears that imprison us. He models an interpersonal style through which he insists on knowing the other, and on being known. (2007, p. 61)

A specific example of Jesus ministering to someone who overcomes shame can be seen in the story of the woman at the well (John 4.4–26). There is potential for shame regarding gender, culture and marital status but she is liberated to testify to the work of Jesus within her Samaritan context. He honours

Zacchaeus (Luke 19.1–10) by calling him by name and going to his house and in so doing helped him overcome this shame through his acceptance of hospitality. Luke 19.7 notes how the crowd murmur about Jesus eating with a sinner in a way that clearly didn't conform with the crowd's idea of appropriate practice for a renowned teacher. Regarding the story of the woman caught in adultery (John 8.1–11), there may have been resonances for Jesus because of what could have happened to Mary had Joseph reacted differently when told she was pregnant. Relating back to different understandings of purity, the acknowledging of personal sin can be seen as signifying integrity and can be perceived as 'a symptom of true wholesomeness' (Collicutt McGrath 2009, p. 52) whereas the Scribes and Pharisees were looking to maintain wholesomeness through scapegoating the woman. Turning to God is the only way to do this.

The story of the cleansing of the leper (Luke 5.12–16) is a further illustration of the willingness of Jesus to associate with those who did not belong in his cultural context. Those watching would have been clear about the significance of what Jesus did because of the statements about leprosy in the Pentateuch (cf. Leviticus 13 and 14). Jesus reaches out and touches the leper and in doing so mitigates the shame that the leper is likely to have experienced. The term 'leper' is still used as a metaphor and some responding to my research felt that was how the church treated them.

While I am drawn to the idea that Jesus predominantly responds to people in a non-shaming way in his pastoral encounters, I am not sure it is universally the case. Thus, in Luke 10.38–42, Martha's behaviour was understandable within the norms of her culture – she was providing hospitality for an honoured guest. Yet when she goes to Jesus to ask for his support in getting Mary to help her prepare the meal, Jesus rebuked her. While commentators differ over whether this was harsh or tender, whatever the tone of Jesus' response, I imagine Martha would have felt shame at her actions in the light of what Jesus said, although some might argue it was guilt. However, within the context of their relationship, it may have been an appropriate challenge that enabled Martha to see her actions in the light of the bigger picture of being a disciple of Jesus. What this story may suggest is that the quality of the existing relationship can make a difference as to how a remark is perceived and whether it accomplishes its purpose of drawing someone into a deeper relationship with Jesus or not. Who the messenger is may be more important than what the message is if we are to hear and receive it; thus taking time to consider who may be best to talk about something with an individual or a group can be worthwhile.

Jesus does tell a story that involves shaming someone. The parable of the friend at midnight (Luke 11.5–13), if seen in historical rather than literary context, does not equate the neighbour with God but as someone who was shamed by not acting in a way that demonstrated appropriate concern about his honour in line with cultural expectations (van Eck 2011). It could be seen as demonstrating how shame may be used as a tactic to get people to comply with expected communal norms, although this can be hard to accept in our very individualistic culture. Thus, this may be an example of Jesus condoning an approach that involves shaming someone, albeit a character in a parable rather than a specific person. Even though it may appear that Jesus did use shaming as a tactic this was in a different cultural context where shame was perceived differently and I still want to argue that it is not normally the most appropriate approach to get an individual to do something or rebuke someone. In what might be seen as his more political dealings where he interacts with those in power, he does more obviously shame them (cf. Mark 11.27–33) and such actions are likely to have contributed to his death.

Jesus' attitudes and principles

The beatitudes (Matthew 5.1–12) can be seen as Jesus suggesting that those who in the cultural setting may be shamed should instead be honoured (Neyrey 1998). Some of the beatitudes led to separation from the social group which was the root of shaming and may have been the experience for some of the early Christians as the Gospel narratives were written.

The list of issues addressed in the Sermon on the Mount encompass some of the many things that can result in experiencing shame. In addressing them Jesus is setting out a way of living that reduces the potential for shame if it is followed. Hospitality is a theme to be found throughout the Gospels. However, Jesus challenges the prevailing culture. Thus, Jesus can be seen as partaking in 'deviant, inclusive, status-leveling, honor-reversing meal practices' (Bartchy 2002, p. 177) through both example and teaching. In Luke 14.7–11 Jesus shames those who seek the seats of honour at the table (the Greek infers a formal banquet) echoing Proverbs 25.6–7. The guests who are mentioned in Luke 14 are very similar to those to whom the good news will be preached in Luke 4.18 and who are blessed in the beatitudes. Jesus disrupted the honour/shame system when he challenged those who sought honour. Those whose dignity he restored through healing or respectful dialogue were given the place of honour. Such a reversal would have been confusing to both groups yet Jesus was clear that the first will be last (Luke 22.24–27). With Jesus there was not a finite amount of honour as may have been believed in the prevailing culture but honour was available to all who sought him. Jesus could give honour to others without diminishing his own honour.

One of the most famous parables of Jesus is the parable of the lost or prodigal son (Luke 15.11–32). The lost son causes his father shame by asking for his inheritance before the father dies, while the older son shames the father by not joining in the party, and anyone observing the father running to greet his lost son would have seen this as a shameful act. Yet Jesus told the story like this demonstrating how shame may be overcome and how perhaps acting in a shameful way that breaks convention is sometimes the most appropriate response. An example of Jesus breaking with convention is the story of the woman anointing him with oil (Luke 7.36–50) where he accepts the act of the woman, affirms rather than shames her and challenges those who would shame the woman.

Another example of this is recorded in Luke 23.29 when he says 'Blessed are the barren.' Familiarity with the Old Testament passages would show that this is a radical statement, as being unable to bear children was a source of shame (Isaiah 54.1) and Jesus destigmatizes this shame albeit in a context where what was once a blessing could evoke great suffering in a time of persecution. In the telling of the parable of the Good Samaritan (Luke 10.30–37) Jesus might have evoked shame in those listening in relation to their attitudes towards people from Samaria.

The death of Jesus

Crucifixion was a shameful way to die in New Testament times. Being stripped naked in front of a large crowd, mocked and tortured before being hung on a cross to die was a gruelling experience, designed to shame. Thus, we encounter a God who 'willingly gives up status and honor, to the point of death, in order to include the excluded and honor the shamed' (Georges and Baker 2016, p. 10). The resurrection shows that the person who was treated so shamefully is the Son of God and Jesus is restored to his former position of honour at the right hand of the Father (Hebrews 2.9). The death of Jesus has such psychological and emotional power because of the way that Jesus embraced the shame archetype through his life, death and resurrection (McNish 2003). He did not engage in the sort of defences normally used such as rage, denial, depression, scapegoating, withdrawal, blaming and so on which helps us to see that we can overcome shame too.

Reflection on Jesus and the Gospels

In exploring the New Testament context and stories of Jesus which relate to shame, there are a range of questions and issues to consider:

- shame and honour were more communal and external in New Testament times than we usually understand them to be today;
- cultural practices and expectations can cause shame and these vary according to context;
- concepts of purity and pollution were prevalent in New Testament times and may still be used today to exclude and shame;
- Jesus saw purity as an internal issue rather than a set of external practices;
- Jesus often broke boundaries and taboos to reach out to heal or engage with people;
- hospitality was central to many of the encounters of Jesus and was used to honour those who may have been shamed;
- Jesus used shaming as a tactic against the political authorities and very occasionally over individual actions which might involve guilt as well as shame;
- the capacity to be challenged in a way that might evoke shame can relate to the quality of relationship we have;
- shaming people for who they are, over things they cannot change is something I don't see Jesus doing, much of his ministry was about acceptance, inclusion, belonging and restoration.
- Jesus bore our shame on the cross and identifies with the shamed, the victim, not those who do the shaming; the death and resurrection of Jesus gives us a new identity as children of God.

Conclusion

In this chapter I have looked at two key biblical themes in relation to shame: the creation narratives and the ministry of Jesus. I have sought to offer perspectives that can inform our ongoing ministerial praxis and that help identify the inappropriateness of imposing on people a shame they do not deserve.

Reflection questions

- Are there any insights in this chapter that are new to you? How do you respond to them?
- In what ways have the creation narratives been used in preaching and teaching in your experience? What is the legacy of this approach to you?
- How do you understand God clothing Adam and Eve? What might be contemporary expressions of this?
- To what extent do an honour and shame culture exist within the contemporary western church or what are the cultural expectations that cause shame?
- Are purity, pollution and taint issues in your context? If so, how are they manifested?
- What can we learn from how Jesus engaged with those experiencing shame about acceptance, belonging and restoration among other things?
- How do we interpret the centrality of hospitality in many of the stories connected to shame? What are the implications of that?
- What is our response to the instances where Jesus uses shaming as a tactic? What are the reasons for that?
- In what areas are we predisposed to feel shame?

3

Personal Shame

Introduction

> *When I was growing up in church I felt unable to be honest about how I lived my life. This led to a dualistic lifestyle, where at home and church I was completely different to at school and with friends. I have felt that church had made me feel like I needed to appear sorted, like I had no issues and that I couldn't be open and vulnerable with people, because if I was, I was rejected or made to feel dirty, bad or shameful!*

While this may not have been all of our experiences growing up in church, it is one I heard regularly during the course of my research. It is chastening to think, as someone in pastoral ministry, that people may not always feel they can be open with me because of (false) perceptions of how I may react. One of the questions I asked was 'What sort of pastoral issues do you deal with that you think cause or are caused by shame?' The responses contained many of the issues we might expect to hear around alcohol, drugs, sex, pornography, eating disorders, self-harm, relationship breakdown, domestic violence and so on. There was also a recognition that sometimes shame was experienced because of life events that were not the fault of the person but that they felt that the church would judge them or their situations. This included such things as suicide, abuse, debt, domestic violence, family members in prison. Issues relating to an abuse or misuse of power were also identified as potentially causing shame. One person summarized their perception by saying '*I believe many of the issues youth workers face are caused by people being ashamed of who they are or what they have done [which is more likely to lead to guilt] and their perceived judgement of this.'* Some suggested that it was church members who were more ready to shame people than the leaders but also that in other instances there was no shaming but people felt that there was: '*I think there is still a stigma that you have to be perfect to be accepted [in church] and I think especially young people who don't attend or won't attend because they feel like they're going to be judged the moment they walk in.*'

As individuals we have different levels of proneness to shame and as someone observed, '*I think that sometimes there are things in your own experience that perhaps make you prone to feelings of shame and you can perhaps . . . be very vulnerable to it.*' That shaming has a long history with the people of God is clear when we read the Old Testament. Bechtel observes that this includes 'making the person a laughingstock, slandering, taunting, scorning or mocking (e.g. 2 Chronicles 30.10; Job 12.4; Psalm 22.6–8; 30.9; 35.15–16; 39.8; 42.10; 44.14; Isaiah 57.4; Jeremiah 20.7; Ezekiel 23.32)' (1991, p. 72). It is debatable whether there are things an individual can do that mean that shaming is an appropriate response. However, what I am talking about in this chapter mainly are the things for which people are shamed that do not merit shaming in that they are personal or cultural practices or actions that are not in conflict with the individual's Christian faith. How Christianity is expressed varies from individual to individual and sometimes we seek to impose our way of being a Christian on others in a way that is unhelpful and which hinders their discipleship rather than enhances it. Dress is a classic example of this. I will try to wear what is appropriate for the context in which I am ministering but if inadvertently I get it wrong, I do not want to be shamed for doing so. I dress in a way which to me complies with any biblical guidance on dress and I want people to feel welcome to come to church without fretting over what are minor details in the bigger scheme of things.

It is also important to realize that in the current cultural climate some Christians feel shame for being part of the church, this response reflecting others: '*Lots of people I know are on some level ashamed of their association with the church. Either because it's seen as not cool, or actively harmful.*' In general, this is not the sort of shame I am discussing in this book but a realization that this is the reality for some people is important as we think about how we present ourselves; hence the comment '*often people don't realize that there are people in the church who hold different opinions to those that appear in the public domain*'.

How do people experience personal shame?

Not everyone experiences shame as a consequence of the things that are said or done which are discussed below, but some do and awareness of this is important in considering how best to encourage an individual on their journey of faith. One significant element is that of feeling judged. One person's experience was '*being judged, excluded and having shame ascribed to me by others. It makes me suspicious of people's reactions to me.*' Kilborne's insight may be helpful here: 'Just as the notion of "grace" designates a feeling that God approves of what he sees, the concept of "dis-grace" designates a feeling of disapproval, an experience of others – who have seen how we have disgraced ourselves – are looking on with contempt and scorn' (2002, p. 6). This can be particularly painful in relation to personal shame although someone helpfully noted the difference between feeling shame before humanity and shame before God and that it was the latter that grieved them most. It is also important to note that bullying can result in personal shame and that the consequence of bullying may depend on what we are bullied over. While bullying may be physical, my experience in the church is that it is more likely to be verbal and manipulative, sometimes with supposed theological underpinning, which again varies by tradition.

Conviction

There may be times when we experience shame because of the conviction of the Holy Spirit – we feel ashamed of something because our involvement in it was dishonouring to God (Georges and Baker 2016, p. 126). Some respondents experienced this through reading the Bible, preaching, penitential times in the Christian year and at the point of conversion. One of the concerns was when others sought to convict an individual where they didn't feel that God was speaking to them or believed God was saying something different.

Unwitting

I want to make it clear that not all shaming (in reality, possibly very little shaming) is intentional. Sometimes we are not aware of what shame is, the impact it may have on people and how our actions can inadvertently shame others. An example given of this was jokes that are made, particularly about things which people may have experienced which are not known to others or assumptions which are made about an individual's circumstances, for example. This story illustrates that tendency:

> *Since I joined the CofE, I've worshipped at a church in a much wealthier part of town. Not long after I joined one of the parishioners mentioned they'd had a motor bike stolen. I said I'd keep a watch out for it – to which came the reply 'well if it turns up anywhere it will be at your end of town'. That was embarrassing for me, they'd drawn the social difference.*

While there is a growing awareness of shame in popular culture and some of us will have been on the end of shaming on social media. There is need for conscientization (Freire 1996), raising awareness in the church context. Some do recognize it, in part perhaps because they know what it is to be shamed:

> *All of us at some time in our lives use this technique . . . Usually shaming reflects my own disappointment and inability to deal with the situation constructively, rather than any reflection on the other person. As someone who was on the receiving end of much shaming in my life, I disappoint myself that it is so easy to repeat the patterns of the past however unhelpful they were.*

Another example was doing something in a new church which was acceptable in a previous church but being told off for it, in this case offering to pray with someone who looked distressed but that was only permissible if you were part of the pastoral team. Once people are aware of how their actions may be interpreted they sometimes change their behaviour.

Difference

Some people experience shame because of reactions (real or imagined) to difference; they don't conform to the norm of the church – as one person commented, '*I don't fit in*'. On asking the question there was a long list of those who don't fit in; examples included divorcees, single parents, people with noisy children, people single past their 20s, those who are introverted, the sick, the unemployed, those deemed too emotional or not emotional enough, those with mental health problems, and those with a partner who doesn't attend church. Other dimensions of feeling different included culture, class, dress, literacy level, where they live, stereotyping, past experiences. Amita observed that some people feel shame because they experience being judged but have no idea what it is that they are doing wrong, as no one tells them. Anna shared something of her story about being a middle-class southerner in a northern working-class urban community. She describes how there was shame around being middle class and recounts that '*I was made very aware that I didn't fit in and I wasn't liked.*' Andy shared how in the affluent northern town where he lives people can be unwilling to say which estate they come from as others will look at them as if they should feel shame because of that. At the other end of the spectrum Simon recalled how a parishioner felt a sense of shame because her testimony was not '*big enough, expressing the sentiment "I love Alpha news but every time I read it, I really wish I was this dreadful scarlet woman"*.' However, another person believes that '*we can generate shame where there isn't any, we can make assumptions*'. Thus, sometimes we experience self-inflicted shame. What was particularly sad was that for at least one person it was easier to be a Christian amongst those of no faith than those of faith because of the '*ridiculous number of subcultures and unacceptabilities*'. While acknowledging that there might be times when shame over difference is self-inflicted in the church, the origins of that shame come from somewhere, a wider culture where there are notions of who or what is in or out. Using sarcasm or humour is an area where one might inadvertently shame people: '*when working with young people who I believe aren't acting their age I might say something like "you're acting like you're five years old". If I'm honest I wouldn't associate that with shame but being made to think about it, now I would.*' This is an example of awareness-raising which may take place when shame and shaming is discussed or included in curricula for training. Humour, banter and similar things can be a source of shame over difference too.

All this suggests to me that as a church we need to work on our capacity to show honour to all and to create a culture of acceptance and belonging. This is not the same as condoning behaviour that is problematic, but it sometimes feels like we condemn for a range of trivial, cultural issues and in doing so can cause people to experience shame which is so debilitating.

Feeling insufficient

Some of us are prone to feeling not good enough and this can be exacerbated through our engagement with the church. The practice of faith is an area where it seems you can end up feeling insufficient. A particularly poignant example of this is feeling shamed for not having enough faith for personal healing; this was sometimes in contexts where a miracle (i.e. an occurrence outside of the usual laws of nature) would have been needed. Bobby, for whom this was the case, was told '*God has given you your healing, it's up to you whether you have the level of faith or not to take it.*' This left him with a strong lack of worth when the needed miracle didn't happen. Those with mental health issues were sometimes accused of not being persistent enough in prayer or not reading the Bible regularly enough. They may also be told directly, or indirectly, that they have demons which need casting out, which can be very shaming too.

The exercise of spiritual gifts was another area – not speaking in tongues when being prayed for to be filled with the Spirit resulted in a feeling of shame for some. Levels of engagement in other spiritual practices also caused shame such as quiet times, personal evangelism or exuberant participation in worship. Such shaming can have a significance, with one person commenting that the shame experienced '*actually made me completely review my whole evangelical background and heritage while at theological college and it was a long time ago, but I remember it as being a very difficult and very, very unresolved experience I think.*' The language of grace, rather than law, is sometimes better for individuals but many of us grew up with 'oughts' and 'should' with regard to our spiritual life and can feel residues of shame if we don't comply with what we were told to do as a 'good' Christian earlier in our life.

Feeling like a nonentity

Experiencing shame can involve a 'dismantling of identity' (Binau 2006, p. 101) and may deplete self-worth (Goldberg 1991). People may feel like a (non)entity through diminution or exclusion. Two of the strongest statements that communicated this were:

- *If you have done anything wrong in your life we will judge you when you come in here. We are goody two shoes and don't tolerate sinners. We will try and change you, then we take your money.*
- *You're not worthy of God's love. You're a dirty, rotten sinner and if it wasn't for Jesus, God would wipe you out.*

Some felt that the church can communicate an exclusivity meaning that you are only okay if you are in or that there is the sense of church as a '*judging presence*' which makes some feel they are shunned. Cliques and snobbery and imparting a feeling of someone being '*less than*' were all reported in the research. One person was actually told that the church leaders didn't like them. Others were made to feel inadequate for who they were: '*I just felt accused of not being what they wanted me to be.*' Some of this is an abuse of power and a denial of what the church should be. Being loved and affirmed for who you are is a very precious gift.

(Non)compliance

Shame can occur over compliance or noncompliance with things which are against our own values or convictions, but we think are expected by the church. Noncomplying shame may occur when we are not able to live up to the ideal self that we have internalized, believing we need to be Christ-like, and feeling like we have fallen short or not measured up. Paul's injunction to 'Be imitators of me, as I am of Christ' (1 Corinthians 11.1) is but one example of how the Bible can sometimes be used to set up expectations of behaviour or activity or gifting, for example, which can cause shame when we fall short. The term Xerox syndrome (Berecz 1998) describes the way that particularly children are encouraged to see Jesus as a perfect example to follow. Referring back to the fall narrative in Genesis 3.4–8, Berecz writes that 'It is in attempting to be "like God" that we generate the highest levels of shame' (1998, p. 89). This can be a danger in certain approaches to discipleship, preaching or liturgy that focus on how we fall short of who God expects us to be if we do not already have a healthy self-esteem that can hold this in tension. A better interpretation for *telios* might be mature or complete rather than perfect or flawless. Romans 5.8 is a corollary to this – 'But God proves his love for us in that while we still were sinners Christ died for us' – suggesting it resembles a Rogerian unconditional positive regard (Berecz 1998).

(Non)conformity

Conformity and non-conformity are issues in shame. For example, one may feel a pressure to conform in ways which are not authentic to oneself or to not conform and feel (or have it inferred that one should feel) there is something wrong because of that. Georges and Baker note that 'Many people raised in Christian circles encounter rules, often implied, about how they should behave. Though it is ironic considering the term, legalism typically uses shame more than guilt to induce certain behaviors, people follow the rules to be accepted by the group' (2016, p. 118). If they don't follow the rules that is problematic. One of the most challenging responses to this was around commitment to and attendance at church. Respondents felt this involved conformity with a set of (usually) unwritten expectations. The concept of commitment includes regular Sunday attendance, time, resources, finance, not meeting expectations (of self or others), lack of volunteering and feelings of inadequacy such as '*generally failing to live up to the call of "being a Christian"*' or that it is '*not OK just to "go" to church*'. This resulted in some people deciding no longer to attend church because they saw no point in going somewhere that made them feel bad about themselves. Susan ended up leaving her church because of their reaction to her saying she needed to pull back her responsibilities on starting University as a mature student. She comments '*I felt quite angry I wasn't going to be supported . . . I thought this person knew my situation. I'd got two teenagers, I was a single parent. I was leaving my job and*

I was going to Uni. It was a big enough step for me'. Another person reports:

> *Various people I know have been shamed for not attending church every week. My minister (in Scotland) has been hounding a friend of mine to meet up with him for months after my friend stopped coming to church – he would be up for tentatively discussing his problems with friends, but feels as though he is being guilt-tripped and shamed by our minister and made to be a 'case'.*

There are challenges in this for church leaders.

There was also a sense of what sort of person was most appreciated by the church and that if they didn't conform to that type they were of less value. Thus, elderly people felt shame when not able to offer as much as they could in the past and had a perception that young people and families were more valuable to the church. Shame was felt by people in relation to their children being perceived as disruptive and not conforming to a standard of behaviour that was often not made explicit.

Another strand of concern was the way that leaders sought to ensure conformity.

This included taking over or usurping authority in a public context, being dismissive, trying to make people look inferior, being accusatory, making false assumptions. One specific example was a new vicar dismissing and devaluing three years' work and then contriving to get the person to leave. This led to the person being unable to connect to church for ten years. Other practices mentioned included oppressive preaching, expecting conformity to a culture: '*a sense that there is only one way of doing things around here*', suggesting cultural rather than biblical standards. Someone suggested '*During times of differing views, some may be made to feel their views or responses to a situation are unworthy of the calling of the institution, even their own calling.*' Forbidding communication with particular individuals or groups of people were other ways conformity was used which induced shame for some.

Other culturally determined areas became the focus of shame for some and while some of this may sound trivial, the experience of shame that some feel over such issues is not so. As one person writes: '*I think there is an unspoken assumption that people should behave a certain way in church, and when that doesn't happen, there can be gestures and sometimes words.*' Thus, people experienced reproach (not always verbal) over picking their nose, farting, children misbehaving, being overweight, being miserable too long after bereavement, choosing a lifestyle that is different though not unethical, being on benefits, tattoos and piercings, unconventional looks or dress, learning disabilities (for parent/carer too), having doubts, suffering domestic violence, being raped, having a family member involved in crime or imprisoned, watching the wrong films or listening to the wrong music. Another person argued that there was pressure on women to behave in certain ways or else feel shame:

> *For women, I think we have to be 'together' or 'sorted', and any sign of weakness or not coping can bring a sense of shame. Women have to be happy to be single, or happily married, wonderful mothers, great friends, and behind the scenes. This is a huge generalization of church, but I would suggest it is the stereotypical attitude towards a woman.*

This was affirmed by most of the women in the focus groups. There may well be equivalents for a range of other groups and reflecting on what messages we send out, what behaviours we affirm is important. I have lost track of how many people have apologized for crying in a pastoral situation despite me always saying that crying is fine and healthy. What values have people absorbed that there may be some shame in crying? There is a challenge as to how we encourage a life of discipleship that isn't culturally determined over issues that have no biblical or theological basis.

One of my concerns in this area is whether shame is preventing people from feeling safe and able to talk about issues that are particularly problematic for them and thus keeping secrets. When I was young, norms and mores involved dress, alcohol, drugs, sex and what one watched, read and listened to; I could feel shame if I transgressed my understanding of what a 'good' Christian girl should do. This may be why some people leave the church: they are expected to comply with and conform to ways of being and doing which they do not experience as authentic. Sadly, what sometimes happens is that shame is self-inflicted, and we can assume that others are making judgements when they are not. Each of us has a predisposition to shame which we bring to our membership of church and it may be helpful to be aware of the situations which trigger us. Thus, I am triggered by issues that I have faced such as childlessness, weight problems and a shyness that is sometimes misinterpreted as standoffishness. They are issues about who I am and the way people sometimes speak, comment or question can trigger shame in me. Others are triggered by comments about their children's behaviour and inferences of not being a good enough parent or an inability to pronounce some of the words in a hymn or not knowing the Lord's prayer when the words are not provided. While none of these things is inherently shaming, some of us are prone to shame in these areas.

Moral and ethical areas

Some will argue that there are things that we might do which merit experiencing shame and these are areas where the Bible is explicit. It is likely that this list would be very small given the variety of areas where Christians interpret the Bible differently regarding what is sin, as well as different views on what takes primacy in ethical decision-making. However, these differences can cause difficulties for individuals: '*I hold what would be deemed quite liberal views of homosexuality and homosexual practice, contrary to what the leadership and majority of my church believe and teach. I have felt unable to voice my divergent views for fear of being overlooked for playing an active ministry role*'.

While all sin separates us from God, within the church there seems to be a hierarchy of sin with sex, relationships and money topping the list. For example, Andrew told of a friend who got pregnant and ended up leaving the church because of judgements from the congregation. One respondent felt shame at the breakdown of their marriage and felt written off. Parallels in the media were mentioned with celebrities shamed frequently but less of a regular focus sometimes on institutions such as governments and banks. Thus, shame often has a personal rather than an institutional focus. A concern was also expressed that if you do fail in a particular area there is not always the support to pick yourself up and continue on the journey of transformation.

Peter's story

'Peter' is someone I have met in real life and I have followed some of his journey on social media. He contacted me in relation to something I posted and offered to share something of his story with me. He was an ordained church minister who had to leave that ministry when his marriage broke down after a very difficult period of increasing alienation from those he was once close to, in the belief that this was important to sustain his marriage. He frames his shame thus and I am sharing it in full as it is another way of understanding shame. He began by emphasising '*I grew up in a loving family surrounded by the best friends and church family. They were and are core to my identity.*' This did not protect him from a difficult shaming experience:

- ***Real shame***
  The shame of hurting my friends and family and the many years of isolation from them, and the further damage, especially to my parents, of missing out on normal grandparenting to my kids. The shame of causing them hurt over a sustained period. The shame of falling into sin personally as

I sought to survive as a human being and find pleasure and love in wrong ways.

- ***Assumed shame***
  The shame of what others might think of me if they knew the things I had done. The shame of what people think of me knowing that I have a failed marriage and failed ministry.
  The shame of what people think of me knowing that I am remarried (In the conservative evangelical world there are some who believe I should now remain single and celibate for the rest of my life having already given my vows to someone). Shame of having failed God in my call to marry and love my ex-wife. There was a deep sense of calling to marry her. I feel like I failed in that calling and let God down in the task he set before me. She needed to be loved. I tried. And I didn't manage it well enough. Shame of my ex-wife running off with another man – different aspects . . . as a man and the sense of impotency this assumes, as an evangelical vicar with the sense of 2.4 children and perfect husband with the perfect family etc., as a public figure and people having the chance to gossip and talk about the vicar and his adulterous wife, as a Christian and feeling I've let God down.

- ***False shame***
  The shame I still feel at the false abusive words my ex spoke over me for 18 years. I know rationally that those words were false, but I still feel somewhere inside me the weight of them and still often struggle to recognize truth from lies internally. I often feel shame about myself when I should not.

His current testimony would be that God is redemptive and restorative and he is dipping his toe back into public ministry. What saddened me was when I asked if anyone in the hierarchy had been helpful as he struggled with all of this, the answer was 'No'.

Responding to personal shame

Fight and flight

Fight and flight are two common responses to difficult situations and there were hints of both of these in the responses to personal shame. Nathanson (1992) offers a model of a 'shame compass' to describe responses to shame which can broadly be seen as fight and flight. On the vertical axis he has 'withdrawal' and 'avoidance' and on the horizontal 'attack other' and 'attack self'. He suggests that the purpose of these four responses is to change the difficult feelings associated with shame. For some people, flight was more appropriate because of the wider consequences for them of fight. This may be because despite their problems with a particular church they feel a broader commitment to it; or, less positively, they do not have the capacity or resilience to act any differently. Phrases used which reflect this include a person describing themselves as a '*quiet rebel . . . without causing too many ripples*', another saying '*I refuse to make my non-compliance an act of open rebellion or controversy*'. However, the internal reaction to this behaviour was difficult for some, such as feeling '*less valued and slightly second class*', or experiencing that '*often there's a screaming child inside giving a different commentary*' and '*[complying] makes you feel like a naughty child . . . you also feel closed in a box and hope that the box can have sides that are open so that you can burst outwards*'. A youth worker talks about how '*This frustration is building within me and I see it as a sign of bullying. When you are shamed for being honest about things (which is often how it occurs) then it suggests there is an inauthentic and unhealthy culture that is not being challenged.*' A measured response was offered by someone who said that '*Nowadays I conform to my conscience, to reasonable demands on me from the church, and to the need not to upset people, but not a step further.*' One of the dilemmas for those who experience shame is that it is possible to get trapped in a negative pattern. In some situations the only possible response seems to be to pray and trust God and some reported the efficacy of that, feeling vindicated by God in the longer term.

Others are more confident in their refusal to comply or conform, suggesting that *'it makes me feel mischievous, more honest and a better Christian'* or it led to *'mirth and rejoicing'*. One individual notes that they deliberately dress how they used to before they were ordained so that they can be who they are not who the congregation thinks they should be as a vicar. The final response made by some is to leave the church because they are not willing to live with the shame that they feel is put upon them or because they are no longer able to live up to expectations, which can be their own as well as others'.

Feeling judged

Another response to personal shame was feeling you were being judged. This was both made clear to and inferred by individuals. Examples included: *'our child ended up feeling ashamed of themselves'*, *'protestors outside our Cathedral for a service celebrating women's priesthood'*, *'being a single mum'*; *'not being interested in speaking in tongues'*; *'told to wear different clothes because my clothes were too revealing'*; *'people from lower socio-economic class being shamed'* and *'more than one occasion of people being treated badly/judged/prevented from being fully involved in church life because they were dating a non-Christian'*.

A particularly sad example is told by another person. Their story reflects how some people choose to believe the worst and judge others when this is without any foundation:

> *When I was engaged we went on a church weekend away and they made a big fuss about us not sharing a room though we were next door to each other. I spent whole weekend feeling that we were having some kind of sordid relationship that everyone disapproved of and that our relationship was dirty. We had never requested to share a room and were not living together before marriage. Felt like we had done something wrong.*

As one person says: 'I think shame messes with our heads, our confidence and our ability to engage fully in life.' The element of feeling judged is common in shame and sometimes it is us judging ourselves negatively.

Theological reflection

Purity

The experience for some is that there are churches that have their own version of purity guidelines (Douglas 1966). If purity guidelines exist, then concepts of pollution and disgust are probably present too. This means that in some churches people feel disgust towards those who have a particular characteristic and it is unlikely that at least some of this will not be experienced by individuals. One of the dilemmas is that this leads to church being, for some, a place where they feel they have to hide parts of themselves and this can mean someone ends up hiding that part of themselves from God too and this may reduce the capacity for healing or wholeness (deSilva 2000, p. 90). The concept of purity can reinforce the idea of shame as being estranging. What we understand purity to mean will impact how we understand shame. Williams asserts that Jesus restored God's original approach to purity, seeing it as an internal heart issue, not an external conformity approach (2010, p. 217). Some of the issues that people experience shame over could be seen as external purity issues such as appearance, political views or social class.

Imago Dei

One of the theological constructs that has been most helpful to me in processing my personal shame is that of the *imago Dei*, humanity made in the image of God. However, inherent in this is the question of the identity of this God in whose image we are made (Brueggemann 2001). This is a particularly pertinent observation in relation to shame and sometimes our responses will be shaped by our understanding of the God in whose image we believe we are made. Thus, for me Schottroff's observation (drawing on the work of Buber) regarding the opening of the book of Genesis that 'The brooding mother-bird with fluttering wings is God's quickening breath, his invigorating and supportive spirit. Furthermore, God's spirit is neither masculine nor neuter, but feminine' (1993, p. 25) resonates in those times when my gender appears to be a source of shame. Taking this maternal image further, God in Genesis 1 can be seen as a mother giving life to her children, she blesses them and then shares the parental risk of letting them grow, develop and try out their power (Middleton 2005). Thus, for Middleton, the implications of the creation narratives is that humanity should exercise power in a loving, generous, non-coercive way seeking to enhance and empower (2005, p. 295) in what may be called a 'hermeneutic of love' (p. 297). This appears to be an apt approach when wanting to respond to shame. While I appreciate that this is but one way of interpreting the creation narratives, it is not solely a more recent feminist perspective. There are writings from the early church that support the idea that Adam and Eve needed to grow and mature, and exercising their free will is a part of that process (Irenaeus 2015).

God's compassion towards the shamed

In thinking about personal shame, another positive perspective is to note God's response to Adam and Eve after they realized that they were naked and hid (Genesis 3.21). God's response was to demonstrate compassion, forgiveness and mercy (Arnold 2008) which might be understood as mediating a God who shares humanity's sorrows (McKeown 2008). God chose to find a way of covering their shame yet beyond this some commentators suggest that in clothing them there was an element of bestowing honour (Wilder 2006). Reassuring for those experiencing shame is that when taking a broad sweep of scripture one may see God as 'not only Yahweh, but also Emmanuel, and who will not leave his beloved creatures to their fates even when they defy him to his face or thrust a spear in his side' (Towner 2001, p. 54). It gave me hope when I began to realize that some of the images of God that I encountered in my childhood were not the only ones to draw on.

Jesus and a community of justice

For those who have experienced shame, that Jesus established a new community of justice evokes hope.

> [He] redirected and redefined shame conventions in which the poor, alienated and dishonoured, including slaves, children, women and gentiles, who enjoy God's glory in the face of Jesus, see God, others, and themselves in new inclusive ways that are not based on blood kinship. At the same time, those who enjoy honour and respect in the public square and in their own kin groups are blinded, and so excluded. In this community of redefined honour and shame, healing miracles, epiphanies and other signs confirm God's reign has begun. (Pattison 2013, pp. 104–5)

Communicating this theological truth is one of the ways in which we can seek to diminish personal shame as we realize that what Jesus did for others, he does for us.

Conclusion

In this chapter I have explored some of the ways in which we experience shame personally and some of the ways this may make us feel. It can be that when we feel like this, shame is at the root but we have never named it. I want to re-emphasise that a lot of shaming is inadvertent and that some people have not thought through the potential consequences of things they say or do. Identifying some of the common responses to shame may also help us in our pastoral encounters with others and assist us in identifying ways of supporting and helping people to process and find liberation from shame.

Reflection questions

- When you read the chapter, which (if any) of the experiences were familiar to you?
- What could have been done to support Peter in his experience?
- What feelings or thoughts were evoked by this chapter?
- Are there any practices or issues that you think may be causing shame in your church? If yes, what might the responses to these be?
- If the chapter has triggered any unhelpful or difficult memories for you, who can you talk to about this?

4

Communal Shame

Introduction

Communal shame is experienced at a group or congregational level. There are three ways this is often manifested: stigma, (dis)unity and (dis)empowerment. Each of these can have theological dimensions or distortions of our identity as people made in the image of God and worthy of honour (Genesis 1.27), the importance of being one as Jesus prayed for us to be (John 17) and the capacity to contribute to the body of Christ (1 Corinthians 12). This chapter has many stories to demonstrate how this is a very real experience.

Anthropological research offers insights into communal shame. Within a collectivist, as opposed to individualistic, context there is often a prevailing style of thought which exerts a strong influence on an individual's thinking, sometimes to the extent that it is not possible to deviate from it (Douglas 1987). Here is one example of this: '*In my old church, if you even hinted that you held people who were different (gay, abortion, different view on heaven etc.) in any esteem or with an open mind, you were definitely frowned on.*' Sadly, there are issues which result in particular groups being stigmatized, and it is common that some people are deemed to be shameful (Nussbaum 2004), although different people will be stigmatized depending on the tradition of a church. We might hope that the church would be different but there were many responses which showed that people felt this was not the case: '*I have this expectation on me to do what everyone else is doing*' and the person felt shame for the way it is implied, for example, that (as another person commented) '*If you love Jesus, you should be on your feet, jumping up and down.*' While this statement may have been exaggerated for effect, some of us will have experienced a pressure to conform to a particular way of worshipping, in part because of what may be thought of us if we are not. It may also be that we want to act in a particular way but for various reasons have not. As Miller observes, 'Shame marks a failure to adhere to communal standards one is deeply committed to; it is the consequence of being understood not to have measured up. It means loss of honor and hence loss of the basis of self-esteem' (Miller 1997, p. 34).

The reframing of the children's playground saying as 'sticks and stones just break your bones. It's names that really harm you' (Nathanson 1987, p. 269) will resonate with some. While sometimes we can dismiss name-calling, it can be experienced as shame as we realize we are not who others hope that we will be or even who we hope we might be. When we stigmatize, we focus on attributes not relationships and sadly we do often use terms such as divorced, single parent, sick, mentally ill as a way to categorize people (Goffman 1990). Being stigmatized and labelled can lead to disaffection, sometimes from others within the particular institution or sometimes more widely. The beatitudes can be read as 'honoured are' rather than 'blessed are' which suggests that Jesus gives value to those who are not usually valued (Neyrey 1998, p. 187).

Within biblical culture, groups are usually the focus, not individuals, and significance and meaning is found in and from the social group that you are part of. My own experience as a teenager was that I was socialized into a particular Christian subculture and that my inclusion and belonging was related to my capacity to conform to that subculture. However, back then I was not aware of that and I doubt that any of my youth leaders consciously saw what they were doing in that way. 'Habitus' is a word we use to describe 'this almost unconscious agreement that here we do things this way' (Moschella 2008, p. 52). If you do not buy into that way of doing things it can be problematic. Sometimes belonging focuses on who we are against as much as who we are. Avoiding name-calling, stigmatization and scapegoating is essential if we are to minimize shame.

Experiencing communal shame in relation to church

Theological tradition

One of the things that happens when I talk about shame is a degree of incredulity that anyone could feel shame about 'that', whatever 'that' is. What became clear was that the theological tradition of the church influenced what caused communal shame. For example, Simon shared how in the church he attended as a teenager there was '*a communal sense of unspoken shame about our failure to evangelize*'. Simon went on to suggest that in his experience evangelical churches tended to be silent about shame and in liberal catholic contexts the shame was sometimes manifested as anger. It is also clear with some of the current debates in the church that what is taboo in one context may be celebrated in another and this can lead to stigmatization of groups or churches by others whose theological tradition is different. Another observation is that '*as with any group of people, assumed consensus is rife in the church – and I have seen and been part of this (on both sides of a fence). My personal experience is that this is especially the case over matters of sexual ethics or attitude towards politics or money.*' It can be difficult if you are the person who secretly doesn't agree with the consensus view. Terms like 'conservative' and 'liberal' can be badges of shame or honour depending on context. The church perhaps needs to explore more fully the impact of unhelpful labelling and debates played out in ways which may come across to outsiders as unloving and stigmatizing, and mediate a God and a church which is off-putting for some. Miller's insights on disgust perhaps help to explain a little the way that groups polarize each other and being aware of this tendency may help us to mitigate it:

> Disgust has other powerful communalizing capacities and is especially useful and necessary as a builder of moral and social community. It performs this function obviously

> by helping define and locate the boundary separating our group from their group, purity from pollution, the violable from the inviolable. It does so also as a consequence of its capacity for being readily experienced vicariously. Disgust, like indignation, is something we experience as much upon hearing and seeing offenses done to another as those done to ourselves. Both emotions seem to compel us to what is often styled the victim's position. (1997, p. 195)

Processes

The processes that we use in church are another area which can lead to disunity and stigmatizing. Responding to change is an area which can be problematic. One person noted how *'The church really needs to begin to understand how to help people deal with change. There is so much learning in secular organizations about how to set about, communicate and lead change, most of which seems to have bypassed the church and then we wonder why people feel insecure, stressed, depressed and bereaved.'* This is an area where many emotions will be involved and they are not all shame but it is helpful to understand how shame may be manifest: *'we assume we all agree that some things are right and others wrong, some people don't want to reorder the building or be involved in fundraising and banging on about it . . . they can feel shame at not catching the vision. It is difficult to voice this difference of opinion – especially if you're on the leadership team as you're seen as not flying the flag'*. It takes time and skill to support people through processes that involve change, but being aware of trigger points, allowing people to voice their feelings and trying to avoid stigmatizing can all help avoid or mitigate shaming. Using people with good facilitation and consultation skills can make a significant difference to the outcomes and sometimes involving people outside the main leadership can draw out more honest responses.

Church practices

When churches promote particular ways of being 'normal' or acceptable then people can feel stigmatized if they don't fit in, and this ranges from minor trivial details to what may be seen as significant theological issues. When much younger I felt shame because I didn't fit the (unspoken) stereotypical woman of my tradition and there were qualities that were more valued than others. One person shared how she was '*told that I would never succeed because I didn't want to speak in tongues*'. Related to this is the danger of a hierarchical style of leadership where members get told what to do and believe, and open exploration or questioning is discouraged. We run a group at church called 'Doubting Aloud' in part to communicate that questions are encouraged, and people are welcome to come and grapple with them without there necessarily being a 'right' answer. One option is to have a box for people to put questions or issues in that can be addressed on such occasions or included in sermons or other teaching. Disproportionate or unjust reactions to disagreement or dissent is also an issue that can lead to people feeling they were being silenced and disempowered.

The way in which we communicate the gospel is an issue with one person commenting that when they were training for the ministry they were encouraged to evoke a

> *response to the Gospel by hooking into people's short-comings i.e. make them feel guilty, highlight their sin, encourage them to consider ways they had let God down. That was the culture. I remember clearly the moment I realized what this was doing to people and rebelled and made a conscious decision to tell people how good, gracious God is, because, on the whole, people already know how imperfect they are – they don't need to come to church to hear that.*

Our theological tradition may again determine how we respond to this example and also to the notion of what it means to communicate the gospel. I am not offering an opinion as to what is right or wrong but encouraging an approach which is mindful of shame and the potential of shaming because of the damage it can do to people and communities.

Another example which may sound trivial but is deeply important to some is shame over the disunity that occurred over a debate about whether to use wafers or bread for communion. Andrew talks about feeling very ashamed that '*as a congregation who is trying to attract young people into the church we are disagreeing about something so pathetic and as a matter of fact we keep forgetting the whole meaning of communion*'. While there may be some who are offended by his statement, as a youth worker he was concerned about the missional impact of such a dispute. In a more mundane example Andy describes how one of the first conversations in church over coffee is not about what God may have been saying through the service but about who is not there, but not discussed in a pastoral way. Christine talked about how the phrase '*nice to see you*' may be used genuinely when people first come to church but ends up being used more ironically if someone hasn't been around for a while. Different expectations over church attendance are often communicated to people even if not discussed directly.

Bad leadership practices

Authoritarian and controlling leaders appear to create an atmosphere where shame is experienced. This may include stigmatizing those with divergent views which can lead to people being removed from leadership or choosing to leave. This was the experience of one person: '*When a preacher/leader from a place of authority rules out a practice as "non-christian", there isn't much else to do but comply if you want to continue with Jesus, is there? Of course, you can always hide your true feelings, but that will often lead to people leaving church, because they can't seem to be allowed to be themselves.*' Related to this was an unwillingness to share views because of the consequences of not toeing the party line. One observation was that

'Leaders who are insecure about their position, and/or their knowledge and ability to be a leader, make others feel they are inferior to him/her, their calling questionable and commitment to the cause or institution not 100%. This is also seen as bullying people into submission.' Generally, the lack of respect for those with different views and the potential or actual stigmatizing of those who are different was an issue. One person saw this as a *'Failure to follow principles of love (i.e. putting the interests of others above oneself, seeking unity above personal rights or selfish interests).'* A more subtle example is:

> *Having been involved in church leadership previously I have been aware of and felt on the receiving end of being shamed. In my experience this involved being asked my thoughts and then being told that they were wrong. I got the impression that they were listening because they asked what I thought but found that my confidence lessened and I withdrew and felt like I was wrong.*

Sadly, some church leaders are manipulative in their approach to trying to achieve a particular outcome and if you collude with, rather than challenge, such an approach that can cause shame.

Another example of manipulation was *'words of scripture used as a weapon and to tell people they aren't suffering, sacrificing, obeying as they should be'*. Judgemental or accusatory sermons were also identified as something which engendered shame in some. One person said that their *'Worst ever experience was when the preacher told us all the Holy Spirit was a he – said in a way that everyone knew they were having a go at me and my friend. Felt like we had no choice but to agree or leave.'* Telling people what to think or do was another concern: *'Last year people in my church were told to vote against a city ordinance that would protect LGBTQ people from discrimination. This happened multiple times, and I had to keep the fact that I voted for the ban a secret because I knew people would give me a hard time for it.'* This was a civil rights issue and the wisdom of leaders telling people how they should vote in a political context is contested; for some it is an abuse of power.

Experiencing communal shame in relation to self

People can feel shame when they believe they have something to offer but feel excluded from particular roles and functions in the church. Thus, '*The church cultivated a culture of haves and have nots, those who were on the leadership track and those who were not. And shame also included not being allowed to be part of the leadership track.*' The pain of being excluded from areas of ministry is very real and some approaches to equipping people for ministry can be quite divisive, particularly if care and support are not offered to those who, for whatever reason, are not chosen. Sometimes there are no criteria and no explanations and it can be very difficult to even initiate a conversation about this divide.

Literacy levels can be another source of shame with people sometimes unwilling to admit that they cannot read and struggle to participate in the service. There is a lack of guidance about how to navigate services where most people seem to know what to do, which book to pick up, when to stand, when to sit and so on. Such things can lead to people feeling that they are not good enough to go to church. But also

> *church leaders/people at the front sometimes inadvertently imply that they are perfect and don't struggle. This can make congregation members who are struggling feel inadequate, ashamed and like they don't belong to this perfect group of people so they hide/leave church or simply put on a brave face but feel ashamed inside.*

While the idea of vulnerability is quite prevalent in some writing about ministry, culturally it varies as to what is expected of leaders and with what they feel comfortable (Nash 2018) which can lead to others thinking they do not struggle.

A more personal story is:

> *As an adult I've never felt I fully fit in in church. I feel uncomfortable when telling other Christians my political and social views even now. I think sometimes I am surprised when I do and it is accepted. I think the church is maybe just not good enough at discussing weakness, at discussing the things we are uncomfortable with and providing space to discuss certain issues rather than just be given a position on them. I have friends in church but not really close ones. I have the feeling that churches don't quite know what to do with me. There is no forum to discuss my views and ask my questions.*

Such a context is very disempowering and many of us can think of people in our churches who may well feel like this.

Experiencing communal shame in relation to others

Dissonance

Communal shame sometimes appears to emerge out of dissonance. Thus, one person reported an experience of a theological college that accepted women for training while not believing in women in overall leadership. Another commented on the mismatch between the denominational standards for belief and local congregational practices and being able to conform to the former but not the latter. The way that Christians segregate according to labels is another area where there is the potential for the dissonance this brings to evoke shame. This is an example at the micro level: '*I have seen churches split or divide amongst the congregation over things as superficial as service times, which technology to use, or whether the priest should wear vestments.*' Others continually feel dissonance: '*I have therefore not ever, even now, felt 100% able to be myself in church as I feel that people expect that when they pray life will be fixed or you should be able to cope more easily and therefore in order not to fail those people or look weak I will often pretend to be okay and this obviously is unhelpful.'*

Attitudes

Attitudes are often communicated non-verbally but many times we get the message. Thus, one person notes that *'if the church lays accusations verbal or non-verbal on people that they "don't conform to OUR norm", or that they aren't keeping the rules/obeying the traditions or they're too sinful or not good enough, then this creates an atmosphere of shame'*. This is explained in a different way by another person: 'W*e are quick to tell people what they are not allowed to do but sometimes fail to follow this up with support for every individual within a worshipping community. Isolation and internalization can easily fuel deep feelings of shame and inadequacy.'* A church member describes the situation like this: '*There is a lot of judgement in the church. People that make assumptions about others' behaviour and say hurtful things.*' This was a recurring theme. '*Feeling judged by others within the church can make one feel ashamed but not really know why? Not feeling accepted by an inner circle can lead to feelings of insecurity and the need for self-preservation/protection.*' Stigmatizing was a practice that was regularly observed or experienced.

Individuals may be stigmatized because of specific cultural values. Thus, Andy talked about growing up in Northern Ireland where the Bible was held in extremely high esteem and as a blind person he would sometimes drop his Bible accidentally and the inappropriateness of this would be clearly communicated. What was very sad, but which resonated with my experience, was a comment that '*I find that people assume that when difference is on the table the church is going to be unaccepting towards difference. I think I found that really exhausting . . . and it would be lovely to see the church not to be the first to reject people because they're different.*' All sorts of attitudes are manifest around difference. For example, Christine was told she was too old to work with children so found a way of doing that outside of the church.

How do people respond to communal shame?

Some people made a conscious decision to sacrifice their own position for the sake of unity, although this is not without its problems:

> *I have often acted to promote unity over and above my personal feelings. When I feel the issue is not a core one, I feel good to be able to put my personal views aside for the sake of the whole, or for the sake of finding unity. But when dealing with core issues of biblical truth, the gospel, sin etc. I feel very uncomfortable. Unity which compromises truth is a false unity. Love does not mean making everyone happy, but doing what is right, and ultimately in people's eternal best interests.*

Another observation was that people lose heart when there is disharmony or disunity as it can feel as if their beliefs are a lie. An interesting response came from one person who finds it '*impossible to promote unity as there will always be someone who is excluded by the actions/direction the church takes so I try to work towards a system of acceptable difference*'. Yet on the other hand someone else suggests that '*I really try to promote unity because I see God working where we as His church operate together*'. A comment from an Asian context was that '*Mostly church leaders are very careful to preserve "face" even of those they don't like, in that to shame someone else risks disharmony.*'

For others, revisiting core principles was important. Focusing on love and functioning appropriately as the body of Christ was one response to stigmatizing and a lack of unity. A thoughtful response about how church and culture relate was this:

> *Sometimes we need to reflect on our teaching and realize the extent to which it has been shaped by cultural norms, but sometimes we need to recognize that the gospel means we become counter-cultural. Yet in doing so, we will induce shame in those who want to hold to Christian faith and practice, and yet live by dominant social norms. So, we have to be careful that we do not induce shame simply because we have not properly thought through our own position, but at the same time be prepared to deal with shame if this is generated by an authentic proclamation and demonstration of the gospel.*

What this latter phrase means is open to interpretation and is perhaps one of the sources of disunity.

Conclusion

There are benefits and drawbacks from belonging to any institution and sometimes the ways we frame belonging means that there are drawbacks for others. As Pattison writes, 'The church may regard itself as a community of sinners, but some of those sinners can be very good at excluding others from the fellowship of grace, sometimes with disastrous effects on individuals and groups' (2011, p. 23). Christianity can be quite tribal which means you are in or out, and sometimes with tribes (think football supporters, for example), attitudes to those from a different tribe are negative. It sometimes seems the closer a community is and the more it has a common ethos, the more likely it is to be guarded by walls and practices of shame, sometimes deliberate, but most often inadvertent and unacknowledged. Once we are aware of some of the issues (and that can be difficult because of the notion of habitus, practices, attitudes, beliefs are ingrained and we sometimes haven't really questioned them) we can look at how we might be less shaming.

Anecdotal evidence suggests that people leave the church because of the shame they experience. We have the capacity to change that.

Reflection questions

- Were there any stories that resonated with you? If so, why?
- Are there any practices in your church setting that would be useful to reflect on in the light of potentially shaming people?
- Have you ever modified or not shared your views because of how others at church might react? How did that make you feel?
- What are the issues in your context regarding unity? Have there been any implications for ministry or mission in your setting?
- Are there cultural dimensions of Christian faith that you are expected to adhere to in your church?
- What norms do you encounter in your setting that might cause shame?
- Are there areas of dissonance for you? If so, how do you process that?

5

Relational, Structural, Theological and Historical Shame

This chapter explores the remaining four dimensions of my typology of shame in the church and are combined in one chapter as they were less prevalent in the stories shared with me.

Relational or vicarious shame

Relational shame is experienced as a consequence of identification with the people within the institution, particularly but not exclusively leaders. This is vicarious shame which is sometimes difficult to identify and name. Relational or vicarious shame can happen across theological traditions but sometimes over different issues as these two contrasting statements suggest: '*political statements by bishops about Tories, Brexit I've seen alienating and shaming people*' and '*I feel shame about the way conservative Christians speak about sexuality and gender*'. As one respondent noted: '*It is often the voices I hear representing the church that bring me the most shame.*' There are biblical examples of relational, vicarious shame. An example of this is when Joab speaks to David about putting shame on the faces of his servants through not recognizing their loyalty (2 Samuel 19.6b–7a). In a New Testament context if one is shamed by others then this wounds both the person shamed and their associates, particularly family (Malina 2011). I would argue that shame contributed to Peter's denial of Jesus (Luke 22.56) as he was not willing to associate with someone who had been arrested or perhaps did not want to lose face with a servant girl. It might also be that Peter chose to return to fishing despite being commissioned by Jesus (John 20.20–29) because he was still feeling shame.

Feeling shame over the actions of others, but not guilt, is something that is observed in wider society. Research shows that 'people were motivated to distance themselves from the event to the degree they felt shame for the other person's actions' (Schmader and Lickel 2006, p. 54). More specifically, 'people felt ashamed for another's wrongdoing to the extent that they felt that the person's behaviour was relevant to a social identity that they shared in common with the wrongdoer and appraised the other person's behaviour as a negative reflection on themselves' and the associated emotional response was to distance themselves. Interestingly the level of interpersonal bonds bore little relation to the shame experienced (Lickel et al. 2005). Some of the big religious scandals over the years can be seen as a result of playing a game of Me Before Anything (MBA), where an individual looks to be seen as a saviour (Mitroff and Pauchant 1990). This can be problematic when someone seeks to replace Jesus as the focus.

Interestingly, Morgan (2008) is a philosopher who believes that we should be able to choose to experience shame in response to some of the dreadful things that happen in the world as this might motivate us to action. Shame is shared with our group, our nation and humanity more widely. 'When we are ashamed, we have lost face because the face we value and hope to have has been displaced or defaced by another face, which is one we regret having, one that disgraces or embarrasses us' (Morgan 2008, pp. 15–16). For many in a church context there is a clear idea both within and outside of the church as to what she should be, or at least a range of understandings as to what is not acceptable. Therefore, if someone who represents the church says or does something contrary to this idea, it may cause us shame.

Bad behaviour of leaders

Various behaviours by leaders caused shame with perhaps the greatest concern over sexual abuse (particularly of children) by church leaders and the subsequent cover-up in many instances.

One person commented on *'the mealy-mouthed disingenuousness of Lambeth Palace in dealing with genuine concerns over Child Protection failings in Chichester. I was so upset I wrote to the Church Times in frustration.'* Another area is extra-marital affairs, with the woman being scapegoated and the male leader restored to ministry at a later date, being an issue for some; this is an interesting take on the Eve stereotype. Generally, issues of corruption, lying and deceit led to vicarious shame when exposed. Vicarious shame is experienced over sexuality on both sides of the debate. Poor preparation for services was mentioned, particularly in civic contexts where this can bring the church or denomination into disrepute. Another example was a counsellor who felt shame over the levels of burnout that happens in the church as it should be an institution which does things differently. Unethical investments by the Church of England were also identified. At a local church level this person had issues with the way the leadership acted:

> *My old church has 'removed' people because they are homeless and therefore 'dangerous' and for having mental health issues, which were also considered to make them 'dangerous'. The church serves coffee during the week, and prices were put up specifically to deter such people. Again, local people knowing I attended this church have confronted me about it, including homeless people.*

Public statements or actions on behalf of the church

When Christians make statements that either are, or are interpreted as being, on behalf of the church (local or national) some feel shame, particularly when there appears to be a lack of grace inherent in the statements or a disconnectedness with contemporary culture or with what are perceived to be biblical values. Some cited the 'No' vote for women bishops in November 2012 as it appeared to be a public statement on how the Church of England perceived women's ministry. An interesting observation was that the *'loudest voices speaking in the name of Christianity often come from the most opinionated and damaging sources'*. Someone else talked about those who behave *'as though you and your part of the church have all the right answers, so no listening is required'*. Problems with exclusion from church and from participating in the Eucharist were also mentioned.

Negative or unloving attitudes

Negative attitudes towards a range of people which may vary according to context and tradition is an area where vicarious shame may be felt. This can include those who are different theologically, by learning style, sexuality, marital status, disability or medical condition, ethnicity, attitude to abortion, dating rules, ignoring or minimizing injustice, historical animosity or divisions between particular groups or denominations; *'morally arrogant'* was a phrase used. Another significant response is:

> *As a women clergy person we are constantly talked about as a 'problem' or 'issue' that has 'divided, destroyed and broken the church'. At times it has felt like we were being publicly named and shamed for daring to be female and a priest. I found this difficult as it resonated with negative experiences of shame in my own life (often a gender issue) so have probably colluded with this by feeling bad about myself and not valuing properly the ministry God has given me to do at times.*

The focus on exclusivity rather than inclusivity and the corresponding apparent lack of humility and tolerance in a range of areas is an issue that causes vicarious shame but women bishops and attitudes towards those who identify as LGBTQI come across most powerfully. Perhaps related to this is an inward focus when so much of the world needs the church to be looking outwards. Historical issues such as involvement in the slave trade and attitudes to immigrants, particularly from the Caribbean in the 1950s and early 60s, triggered vicarious shame in some. Some other specific behaviours mentioned included abuse of power, putting people down, criticizing, lying, seeing people treated as *'little people'* by the hierarchy, bullying, transference, misuse of confidential knowledge, martyr spirit, controlling through theological knowledge, imposing cultural values on people, public humiliation. An example encompassing several issues is:

> *I personally feel this at times when I continuously try and keep in contact with those that have left the church for various reasons e.g. a pregnant lady who has no partner, a couple who publicly challenged how the church uses their finances and someone who married their same sex partner. I feel the continuous need to include them as part of conversations with the hope that they will one day return to worship. I am often then left feeling hopeless as others seem to disregard and further stigmatize.*

Cultural images

For some the popular image of clergy, particularly on television, as *'ineffectual, elderly, naff'* may evoke vicarious shame. Clergy are presented in *'amusing and embarrassing ways'*; as one person said, *'I feel shamed by the perception of ineffectual half-baked clergy really if I'm honest, as I am one'* (which was not a fair reflection of this person but they demonstrated a residue of shame from various experiences).

Responding to relational and vicarious shame

The main concern here was the perception of the church and God to those outside of the church, particularly friends and neighbours. Thus, one person responded: *'I feel it because I am identified as "the church" by people I know who are not Christians, and it makes it harder for me to have sensible conversations with them as they think I share church attitudes.'* '*Tainted by association*' was another way of putting it. Comments ranged from the church being perceived as '*out of touch*' or irrelevant, acting in a way that is '*so much the opposite of what Jesus would want us to do*', lacking credibility, being complicit in stereotyping, hurting people, what happens at a local level being tainted by national pronouncements, being seen as judgemental. Some wanted to take ownership of what happened, acknowledging that '*I feel part of the church and therefore its failings are mine.*' The vicarious shame that is felt can lead to further questioning of self: '*a friend supported an international figure with money and time. It turns out that dodgy dealings were highlighted and this brought enormous shame as well as questions about did God really lead me, or was it just me, should I have known?*'

Structural shame

Structural shame relates to shame that is a consequence of what the church or organization says, does, or believes at an institutional level. Many of the comments that were made in the research were around collusion and fragmentation in how potential problems were addressed. The anthropologist Mary Douglas argues that institutions can 'think' and they construct a 'machine for thinking and decision-making on their own behalf' (1987, p. 63), representing their understanding of how things work. She then suggests that the consequence is to seek to impose order on untidy experiences using concepts such as purity, separation, punishment for transgressions and boundary-setting (Douglas 1966). For some this is how the church works in their experience.

In Matthew 16.15 Jesus asks his disciples 'But who do you say I am?' The way that institutions and churches operate structurally offers an answer to that question. Jesus is mediated through structures and systems as well as people. In some settings there appears to be a dissonance between the Jesus who is preached and the Jesus who is embedded in the structures. A pertinent observation was made in a focus group: *'There's this apparent and, I think, often true, genuine, wholehearted acceptance of people in the beginning, and then the rules kick in'* when the structure determines practice. This was a recurrent theme; Paula suggested that people end up being shamed because *'Perhaps they can't do what's being expected of them. Perhaps they never were going to be able to do it. That's where the relationships start to break down.'* Some of the prophetic literature addresses the issue of shame and looks forward to the hope of God removing the shame and restoring the honour that had been lost in the exile. For example:

> I will deal with all your oppressors at that time.
> And I will save the lame
> and gather the outcast,
> and I will change their shame into praise
> and renown in all the earth.
> At that time I will bring you home,
> at the time when I gather you;
> for I will make you renowned and praised
> among all the peoples of the earth,
> when I restore your fortunes
> before your eyes, says the LORD. (Zephaniah 3.19–20)

Church practices

The practices of our denomination have the potential to cause us shame. One area where this is experienced is the selection, training and deployment in denominational churches and the lack of pastoral care for those who are hurt by the system. This is one of several examples:

> *The system of appointing leaders to churches is not a system that encourages conversation – so a refusal to accept a given appointment or to question its appropriateness would*

be responded to by the suggestion that there was a problem with their relationship with God . . . Overall, the denomination has a very parental attitude to its leaders and members and seems to encourage and prefer it when they remain in Child mode. Seem to struggle to work Adult to Adult. (Transactional Analysis terms, see Hay 1995)

Another area was prescribed services and prayers where you end up colluding with a view of God or oneself that is hard to hold with integrity with your personal views. Anglican clergy having to say the office twice a day was also identified as a structural issue that can cause shame for those who do not comply.

Structural understandings of leadership (which may also be theological) can also exacerbate shame, with senior leaders believing they need to know everything that goes on or have a God-given responsibility for them (as in the Anglican cure of souls). This means that confidentiality is often conditional (beyond safeguarding guidelines) and sometimes this is not explained and individuals can be surprised when an issue gets raised by another. This story is perhaps the most extreme example but shows an approach likely to cause shame: '*After our vicar had found out that the woman's 16-year-old daughter had had an abortion he said something to her along the lines of "How's your daughter feeling now she's killed her baby?"*' The structural organization of the church ended up with an individual being shamed and is an example of the poor keeping of confidentiality and an abuse of the way the cure of souls works.

The dissonance between what is said at a structural level and what may be done in reality was a frustration for some: '*demanding conformity – and using "doublespeak" much like the government, where they say they embrace diversity and welcome all (for example) but behave differently . . . where they talk about prophetic words and action but do not speak on behalf of most marginalized people unless it serves their agenda*'.

While there are genuinely held doctrinal or ecclesiological differences, the fragmentation in the wider church that can occur through these may be a cause of shame. At the extreme these have led to the evolution of new denominations. An unwillingness to accept that there are a range of acceptable perspectives on a particular topic can be problematic.

Power

Some experienced what they saw as inappropriate uses of power. For example, '*Hierarchical structures and expectations of leadership not being questioned – they are, after all, appointed by God – leads to guilt and shame.*' One person commented: '*I do see shame being used as a means of getting, not deference, but someone to toe the line.*' Anna shared what she perceived to be an abuse of power, causing her shame, when her church leaders told her that she should go back to a mission situation where she had been spiritually abused and suffered a serious sexual assault as this was God's plan for her and in returning home she had failed and needed to go back. Ten years on they still believed their position was the right one and that she was not on plan A for her life. Someone else talked about how their affluent church had been working with those with alcohol, drug and mental health issues but problems began to emerge when those they ministered to wanted to participate beyond the carefully prescribed boundary of a specific event. The consequence was that the archdeacon rang the vicar commenting that '*Well, of course, you realize wealthy people need the gospel too, don't you?*', trying to put pressure on to keep the work boundaried and away from other parts of the church ministry.

Cultural issues

Denominational approaches to such issues as sexuality and gender cause structural shame, on both sides of the discussion. Some believe their denomination is too accommodating to culture and others not responsive enough although this may be expressed in theological language. An interesting observation was made that shame can depend *'on what expression of church you attend; there are different hierarchies of shame depending on what that particular expression of church prioritizes in regard to teaching and culture'*. Another person noted that *'Much of what the church does in this matter of shame is unintentional but reflects a culture within rather than a purposeful shaming or judging.'* Structurally the leader may also be prone to shame as it can be hard to live up to the expectations of the role.

How do people respond to structural shame?

At the extreme, people respond to structural shame by leaving the church, either the particular local church or sometimes the institutional church. Others switch denomination to find one which is more in keeping with their values. The levels of dissonance that institutional pronouncements and actions can engender can cause significant stress to people and choosing to either collude or not collude and thus confront church hierarchies is a difficult decision.

Theological shame

Theological shame relates to institutional belief systems and the way in which theological beliefs can engender shame. Thus, people experience theological shame when their view of God or their core beliefs are challenged, oppressed, ridiculed or misrepresented. One church member made this observation which reflects the frustration that came across in the research with the way that God is mediated:

> *I think that often the church forgets the real meaning of grace, the fact that there is nothing anyone can do to make God love them more and nothing they can do to make God love them less. God is often portrayed as up there keeping an*

> *eye on us, watching our every failing and sin, rather than a loving God who longs to spend time with us, commune with us, lavishly pour out his love on us.*

In looking at theological shame I found the concepts of dissociative and associative shame helpful and understand them in this way: associative shame may arise when we are identified with a particular theological position which is regarded negatively by some, whereas dissociative shame can occur when hearing a theological position being espoused that we cannot hold to. Some found it very easy to identify the ways in which theological beliefs can lead to experiencing shame and this quotation gives a flavour of the breadth of responses:

> *I think there's a lot of theological shame directed at women who don't conform to patriarchal assumptions about faith. Also a lot of theological shame is placed on girls and women through purity culture. I think there is also much shame around theological teaching around sexualities. I think the gifts of the spirit can be used to cause shame if people do not manifest them in the way the church has deemed acceptable. Also people with health problems may be shamed if they are not healed. I think men are often shamed by theology around masculinity and men who don't fit into those models are shamed for not being 'man enough'.*
>
> *Conservative evangelicals are often shamed for their beliefs, othered and treated with unkindness (for the record I am not part of a conservative evangelical church).*

Appearing unloving

An example of such views is this: '*We are always seen as what we are against – women bishops, gay marriage are the current ones, but there have always been loads. So the Christian church is not seen as being open armed. Jesus gives us two commandments: to love God and love people. I am ashamed that we are not known for either of those.'* An unhelpful emphasis on a God who punishes is seen as potentially dissociative; an associative approach is teaching and liturgy that reflects Jesus as portrayed by the Gospels. One succinct response was: *'Anything the church does that excludes will lose me every time'*. Grace came through as a theme in some of the responses in this area.

Doctrinal differences

Approaches to baptism were one area raised here with some strong disagreements between those who baptize children and those who baptize only adults. People had also experienced theological shame personally through a perceived lack of experience of the Holy Spirit or taking a different stance on the Bible. *'Potentially, the heaven and hell issue is still a major source of finger-pointing'* or accusations of being a universalist which for some is a term of shame but for others honour. Someone commented that *'In my diocese things are presented as gospel/salvation issues as a way of ensuring compliance; e.g. I can't support women's ordination or gay relationships and be a Christian. Yes, I support both these things. But I tend to keep it to myself. Not feeling safe is the result.'* Again, there was significant comment about gender roles and sexuality which could be categorized under this heading. There were comments about women being treated as second class and not being forced into stereotypical roles, as well as the 'No' vote to women bishops in the Church of England in 2012. Correspondingly there was this response about what causes shame:

> *The theological view that it's OK to re-interpret the Canons in favour of ordaining women and then marginalizing or bullying male clergy who don't agree with the ordination of women and subjecting them to a routine of bullying and intimidation making it impossible for them to take up for fear of reprisals as when people like Philip North are offered key positions such as Bishop of Sheffield and feel they can't accept the position.*

One of the topics that evoked the strongest opinions in this area was people's experiences of healing and deliverance. Thus, '*I was once told that I didn't have just one demon but a whole hotel of them. Also, really destructive to be asked to come up to the front and confess sins in front of the whole group in order to receive healing.*' It is quite easy when in a vulnerable position for people to experience shame that they are inferior, lack faith, have sinned in the past or done something else which the person ministering infers has resulted in the ministry not being successful. Those with physical and mental health issues that are not seen as medically curable sometimes find themselves accused of a lack of faith which leads in some to feeling shamed. This was seen as leading some people to leave the church or to find a church where they could be more anonymous.

Teaching on sexuality, women in ministry and divorce were areas of doctrinal difference. There were many responses on these topics such as '*complementarianism is often expressed as anti-women; gender and sexuality issues are often clothed in real bigotry or careless language. People feel unable to express dissent or even question the received wisdom of the wider church.*' There was agreement that churches have a hierarchy of sins although theologically that can be hard to argue. As suggested above, people may feel dissociative shame partly in relation to their theological tradition as different things are particularly shameful. I had a fascinating brief conversation over which coffee shops it was appropriate to go to if you were a left-wing liberal Christian. Simon suggested that in liberal catholic churches the top sins are to do with poverty and politics but within evangelicalism it is generally sex. Andy recalled how the biggest obstacle to him potentially getting a job appeared to be that his wife then smoked. Jackie, who is in ministry, told of how a couple of friends made a joke about her maybe being a prostitute as she was so secretive about what her job was and her fear had been that people would assume she had a negative attitude towards sexuality as she worked for the church.

A significant concern in this area is the way that the Bible has been used to justify abuse within the church and the way some women in particular have been encouraged to return to abusive husbands based on a doctrine of submission. Approaches to the Bible can result in people being shamed and Susan told of her mother who was told she couldn't be a good Christian if she didn't believe in the literal truth of the Adam and Eve story and how she has never gone back to church because of the attitude displayed towards her.

However, for some the failure to adhere to biblical teaching was an issue:

> *I cannot condone or conform to any practice or belief which contradicts Scripture. Obviously there are issues of interpretation and a lot of 'grey area' but in some cases, Scripture is blatantly disregarded in favour of personal freedom, tradition, human rights, the idea of revising Scripture for the modern day, or a half-truth of God loves all of us just the way we are.*

Characteristics of associative churches

The characteristics of a church that people wanted to be associated with included the following: loving; build community; caring; connected; a concern for the world; believing that everyone is equal in God's eyes and acting as if this is true; committed to salvation, the poor and the environment; faithfulness to the gospel; articulates a hope for the future; believes that God created us for a purpose; engaged in mission; gospel of grace and love; presenting an accepting, loving God; contributing to society.

Characteristics of dissociative churches

The characteristics of churches that people wanted to dissociate from included an unwillingness to embrace diversity;

intolerance; bigotry; unkindness; inability to make decisions or non-consultative decision-making; judgementalism; stinginess; fractiousness; self-righteousness; prioritizing structures and institutionalism; focus on externals rather than loving relationships; hierarchies; leaders whose default is critical parent; distorting scripture.

How do people respond to theological shame?

For some people again the response is to leave the church. Others are concerned with building a church that reflects their view of who God is. The fight/flight paradigm can be relevant here for some people. Others are part of an institution and make choices depending on what their hopes and expectations are in relation to the institution. Both cognitive dissonance and denial may be experienced in relation to theological shame and perhaps some of the responses to child sexual abuse by denominational leaders reflects this, which exacerbates the horror of what occurred.

Historical, buried or residual shame

Historical shame relates to issues in the past where there is still a residue of what happened embodied in particular people or a group. 'Whether it be by explicit decision, implicit agreement, collusion, or a combination of these, communities sometimes decide never to tell the whole story and to keep some past event hidden at all costs, which can lead to rigidity of role, stuck interaction patterns and close monitoring of storytelling to ensure the secret remains safe' (Whitehead and Whitehead 2003, p. 17). This can particularly be an issue for new people who are not told about it but can sense that something is wrong. This can be an area that is dealt with poorly by the relevant authorities and there is often little support or skill to explore it from the perspective of those affected by whatever the issue was.

An example is: *We had a secretary run off with a church member (breaking a family). It was as if it never happened. What was astonishing was that the wife and children of the adulterous husband were shamed! They eventually left – sadly.*

An illustrative comment is: '*There is always an unspoken wariness which raises its head now and then. People wonder about it, can feel it but often don't know what it is.*' Issues that tended to be covered up included sexual misconduct, mental health issues, abuse, bullying and poor decision-making. Sieff notes that 'In some instances the original painful experiences happened to previous generations rather than directly to us. In these cases it is the hidden fears and distorted ways of relating that our recent ancestors developed which are surreptitiously and unconsciously passed on to us' (2015, p. 2). In reflecting on the research both buried and residual shame are relevant when looking at historical issues. I differentiate them thus: residual shame is the part that remains after an incident is over or has been partially dealt with, whereas buried shame is more a term for shame that has never been properly dealt with. An example of residual shame came from a female priest who wrote: '*Many of us have to remind ourselves that we do not have to apologise for our existence or our calling . . . Seniority of post can increase this rather than diminish it.*' In a similar vein, Reddie suggests that 'The issue of shame emerges as a knock-on effect from the existence of racism. The need to counter the worst excess of racism has led many Black communities becoming neo-conservative enclaves where the dictates of "doing the right thing" or being seen to do it takes precedence over other concerns' (2019, p. 118). Whereas this sounds like buried shame:

> *When I worshipped in a small community, I once asked the pastor why there were three churches serving the same small area. No real answer was given but later I found out that a number of the church leaders were once core leaders of another of the churches. There were disagreements on how the church should move forward and some then split from the church and created their own. For years there was a*

divide in the village and to this day, there is still a cloud over when happened 25 years ago.

One emotive term is 'clergy killers' (Knudsen 1995, p. 81) used to describe what may happen with a congregation where issues have been suppressed and kept secret. An associated term is 'toxic waste' (Knudsen 1995, p. 83) and the way people act out to cover up a sense of shame or violation because of what may have happened in the past. Another respondent talked of what could be called '*congregation killers*':

The church where leadership made a bad decision, stuck with it, and forever refuse to go back and repent of that action, rather sticking to their prerogative as leaders with authority, than servants with loving responsibility. Often a church can never progress because of this buried shame. It lies dormant, undealt with, and even continues to simmer into the next generation.

In other contexts, there may be a lack of awareness of the buried shame which still impacts current relationships. Thus, one of the respondents to the survey noted how

a big picture example is the revision of the Nicene creed by the addition of the filioque clause (by unilateral decision of the Western church) and the resulting final split with the Orthodox. Even the protestant and evangelical churches have inherited this split, which remains at the core of the Orthodox grievance, yet no one can seem to find the will to repent of it for the sake of unity.

This comment demonstrates the potential for buried shame at structural levels too. This is reinforced by one of the respondents to the survey who noted: '*Some of the abuse issues of the past bring out buried shame, such as the role of the church in the stolen generations of Australian aboriginals, the pattern of enforced migration of British children to the colonies or sexual abuse of children through church institutions or individuals in positions of power.*' Such resistance to acknowledging or dealing with these issues can be negative for the particular institution as well as the wider one. Fortunately, some churches are willing to engage with shame rather than burying it. In a focus group one person told how a church avoided the worst of this after two leaders ran off with each other. The church took note of prophetic words which encouraged trusting in God. They owned what had happened and tried to learn from their mistakes and in that owned the shame. It is much less likely that this incident will be hidden from future ministers who may not otherwise understand what is going on.

How do people respond to buried shame?

Some people, seeing how the church responds to such situations, are reluctant to confess to anything as churches seem to find it so hard to deal with shame-related issues. One of the difficulties in not dealing properly with such issues is the way that '*unresolved resentments, hurts and shaming can lie and fester, or cause people to withdraw*'. Another person noted that after incidents of infidelity in leadership or mistreatment of leaders there can be a climate of mistrust in generations of church members. A similar point was made with the suggestion that '*The church or new individuals that do not know of the hidden shame often have to deal with the fallout from this shame without knowing why there is conflict and thus how to resolve it.*' Moschella offers some helpful advice around how to approach such things:

> When a group recalls and tells its painful history, allow for the expression of that pain through some poetic or expressive means. For example, when a congregation comes to terms with the sexual misconduct of a previous leader, the people may speak of trauma, loss, betrayal, or shame. Try to respond in a way that allows the group to process the emotional burden of this event in their history. This might

involve singing a hymn of mourning or reading a Psalm or a poem that captures the anguish and expresses it. When a group has endured such a breach of faith, the outcry must be uttered, maybe in a way that is too deep for words. (2008, p. 231)

Finding ways to help process things at the time they occur is much more helpful than having to try to facilitate healing from things that have happened in the past.

Conclusion

The four areas covered here are the less obvious manifestations of shame in the church but each can have a significant impact on our experience of the church as a visitor, member or leader. The areas that are reflected here can be detrimental to our witness, our mediation of God and result in accusations of hypocrisy as the church seeks to speak out on some topics while struggling to handle her own issues. Sexual abuse is an issue in relational, structural and historical shame and may also have theological roots. It is an issue that continues to shame the church and one where there is no dispute that this is a shameful and shaming activity. The lack of material on sexual abuse in this book is a reflection on the questions I asked people in my research in trying to uncover more covert and less obvious shame; it is not a reflection of my views of the abhorrence of the act and the inadequacy of some of the associated responses.

Reflection questions

- Have you ever felt vicarious shame? If so, over what?
- What are the key issues over which you may experience shame?
- Are there things which happen at a denominational level that you struggle with?

- What structures do you find helpful and unhelpful in your church experience?
- Which theological issues do you feel most strongly about? Where are you able to discuss them?
- Are there theological issues that you feel impact the mission and ministry in your church?
- Do you have any experiences of buried or residual shame? What has been the impact?
- How are issues of shame dealt with in your church? How could they be processed to have the least impact on future ministry?

PART 2

Confronting Shame

6

Shame, Liturgy and Ritual

Introduction

Whether or not we are aware of it happening, worship, liturgy and ritual are instrumental in shaping our understanding and identity of ourselves as Christians and our view of God. This can be both positive and negative. I am grateful to a colleague, Daniel Corcoran, for reminding me that 'How is this understood?' is a really important question that we need to ask. Thus, thinking about who is in our context and their starting point may lead to a different answer to our own. Therefore, the content of our liturgy and ritual is important, particularly the language and concepts that we use so we might not 'inadvertently blow out that smouldering wick or break that bruised reed. The person coping with unhealthy shame is a very vulnerable person' (Watson 2005, p. 22). There are many ways in which shame can be triggered, including how confession is done, regulations around receiving Holy Communion, the use of concepts of dirt and defilement, the idea of a perfect all-powerful deity and what happens to those who do not conform to the image of what a child of God is supposed to be like. The language used can be challenging for those who are shame-prone with ideas of purity, submission, obedience, humility, being a sinner, unworthy and so on, reinforcing already negative self-images. Some of what I write may sound over-sensitive but my main purpose in writing this book is to raise awareness of how we inadvertently or unthinkingly shame, and I am minded to try not to put stumbling blocks in the way of people following Christ (Romans 14.13).

Experiencing shame in worship

> *It took me some years to start attending church because of what I perceived to be the complexity of liturgy and ritual. I can still feel 'wrong footed' in this area, especially in an unfamiliar church.*

This response suggests that the area of liturgy and ritual is one which needs careful consideration in relation to shame. While for some, a trial and error approach, without worrying if you get it wrong is fine, others can feel quite sensitive about being in a new situation and could experience shame at not knowing what to do when it seems everyone else does. I felt distinctly awkward when experiencing Holy Communion one-to-one in a hospital chapel as I was clearly from a different church tradition to the priest and I felt like I was not doing things right. I know I can be prone to this and had I been a long-term patient I may well have avoided going back because of those negative feelings. Such feelings will not be shame for everyone; in relation to church there can be a feeling of 'I am not good enough', which is often a shame-based response. One person shared: '*I was in a church context where people were encouraged to attend communion as family groups and the importance of family was emphasised. I know for me and other single people in the church this felt quite alienating and uncomfortable.*' Much of what happens is not intentional and it is inadvertent shaming that I am trying to raise awareness of. Sometimes when people don't come back or stop coming, shame or other negative emotions can be a significant cause.

Daniel Corcoran, in private correspondence to me, offers an analysis of why liturgy and worship is difficult from his many years of experience ministering in areas of multiple deprivation:

> *Working with many hurting individuals and communities over the years I have had conversations and thoughts about church expressions failing to scratch itches and heal*

wounds. Churches (of all traditions and denominations) seem to display unhelpful patterns which keep the gospel scratching-stick away from itches, preferring to miss opportunities to bind broken hearts in favour of sounding as if we can't quite take God at his word. Pragmatically, this has a lot to do with 'Proclamation' vs 'Precatory' style: how at times we proclaim the promises of God happening now and how at others we pray for these promises to happen. From experience, the former lifts from the miry clay and sets feet on solid rock and the latter creates uncertainty and doubt leaving those drowning in shame (and guilt), still drowning, largely due to such liturgy being meddled-with Scripture cut and pasted and passed off as liturgy and worship regardless of its original context and meaning. For instance:

- *We use David's 'take not your Holy Spirit from me' (Psalm 51.11) causing needless worry leaving people feeling 'that's probably why I feel so bad!';*
- *our endless requests in prayers and worship songs for our Emmanuel God to 'be with us';*
- *our obsession with David's request 'hear my [our] prayer' which Jesus doesn't deem important when teaching his disciples to pray.*

I am not suggesting that we should stop asking God for things! However, I am suggesting that liturgy should reflect a 'present your requests, with thanksgiving' approach (Philippians 4.6): thanking God for the gospel-givens which God provides rather than praying for them. Unfortunately, I sense a huge and unnecessary chasm between the sure and certain givens-of-the-gospel on one side and the church's uncertain 'Not-sure-these-are-givens' on the other presenting the gospel as ineffectual.

There are three particular areas that Daniel identifies as problematic in this regard: the way we portray God as inactive, the liturgical obstacles to prayer and not offering a clear absolution; some of this will be explored below.

I was talking to a bishop in his cathedral and he pointed out the bishop's chair – up some steps looking down on everyone. He explained how he only used the chair for his enthronement as that was required but had not sat there since. The way that a building is set up can communicate quite powerfully to people, thus, '*The preacher, the worship leader, the people on the stage, are quite literally, higher than the rest of us, and I think this sinks into people's subconscious.*' This can lead to some inappropriate responses which can include an unhealthy deference or hero-worship or failure to accept that leaders are flawed humans too with the potential to abuse their power.

One of the delights of my journey with researching shame is when people contact me offering to share their story. Peter's experience helps us to see that responses may not be consistent and that the journey out of shame may be a long and complex one:

> *I think for me the honest truth is that it all depends what day of the week it is as to how I respond to worship in church. Some days it warms my heart, other days I walk out of church feeling broken and alone. The worst aspect of church for me is the constant proclamations of God's goodness, his good plan, his power to perform wonderful deeds, etc. All this says to me is that I have ended up so far outside of God's will that the chaos I've endured has been because of my sin. The truth about my shame in this context though is that it waxes and wanes. There is never one Sunday when I feel the same as any other Sunday. Sometimes my feelings and experiences can be wholly opposite from one week to the next. I guess that's part of the mental health journey many experience.*

The language used here by Peter has been shaped by a particular hermeneutic and what we have been taught, particularly perhaps in childhood or adolescence or in our early years as a Christian, often lingers on, sometimes unhelpfully. Thus, domestic abuse victims are sometimes encouraged to stay with a violent partner because that is what a good Christian wife should do, this being the way obedience and submission are taught (Collins 2019). We are encouraged to see Jesus as a perfect example to follow (based on Matthew 5.48, which encourages us to be perfect as the Father is perfect). This verse highlights one of the dilemmas of English translations of words that are more nuanced in the original Greek. Here the idea of maturity as a process may be more helpful than perfection as a defined state we all fall short of. It was in trying to be 'like God' that Adam and Eve encountered shame (Genesis 3.4–8) and our endeavours to be perfect may cause us to experience shame too. There is also a danger that this leads us to label others as impure, defiling or not good enough. Worship as an opportunity to tell yourself how bad you are and that God agrees with your judgement is not helpful for those who are shame-prone and will condemn themselves for things which God would not. The perceived inactivity of God feeds into this as well. Daniel writes:

> *Some may be equipped with sufficient church literacy to be able to ask for God's love and presence while knowing we are assured of it. This benefits a privileged few rather than those predisposed to negative thought patterns. And of course wider society would naturally presume that such a request meant that God's love and presence is only with those who ask.*

Trigger warnings

One of the dilemmas with shame is that we sometimes think we are the only person who is experiencing this. There may be material in church services or rituals that could trigger shame and I rarely hear a trigger warning given. What giving a trigger warning does is show that leaders are aware that there are some who may be sensitive to the content but this can help in feeling we are not alone in experiencing shame. It can also open up some conversations about how we understand our faith. We also might find it helpful to have an awareness of triggers in our minds when we prepare worship. At our church we have two people available to pray after the service for anyone who would like that; it could be that in some weeks we want to be specific about some of the things people may value prayer for after that particular service.

Metaphors

Metaphors are much used but can be problematic. I responded to an altar call and experienced a repentance-based conversion which led to be being 'in' not 'out', and I became part of the family once I too was baptized by full immersion. Family as a metaphor can be challenging, as in most churches there are some of the dysfunctions of a family and not all feel a sense of belonging. But family metaphors also have implications when, for example, someone is excluded from taking Holy Communion, the psychological message this sends can be very unhelpful. How God is mediated as father is unhelpful for some who do not have a model of a loving father to relate to. What we understand by such terms as 'bride of Christ' (Revelation 19.7–10), 'body of Christ' (1 Corinthians 12) or 'army of God' (Joel 2.11) may depend on a range of issues about who we are and our ability to embrace such metaphors. In pastoral encounters I have found that some struggle with the concept of the bride of Christ as it reinforces a sense of shame, disappointment or failure that their own marriage breakdown evoked or a disappointment at singleness, for example. Body image is an area where there is much discussion and what part of the body we feel like can be positive or negative for us. 'Army' is perhaps a more controversial term to suggest as a trigger but it can sound a little too militaristic and have echoes of some of the worst practices of Christianity in colonialism, insensitivity or bullying, or extreme acts carried out in the name of Christ. Given they are metaphors we find in scripture, it may be that we continue to use them but perhaps when doing so acknowledge that there are limitations which make them difficult for some.

Worship

One of the issues with worship is that sometimes it feels like Freire's (1996) critique of a banking approach to education. As Amita said, '*you come and you get your fuel and off you go. It runs out at the end of the week, so you come back again. It's not a case of take it, chew on it, think about it, come back to me with it, can we talk about it?*' This means that more complex issues such as shame are often not explored because of the time thoughts may take to process and also because of a reluctance to want to talk about personal or deep issues. Many people feel it is shaming even to talk about shame.

Our disposition when we facilitate worship or ritual is significant. Those suffering from shame may be vulnerable and there is the potential for this to be exacerbated by inappropriate liturgy or ritual. What is important is being present, demonstrating grace, humility and servant leadership.

Elements of the liturgy

Churches vary in their approach to liturgy. As an Anglican priest there are guidelines within which I need to work and I choose not to use some options because they induce shame. However, shame is so individual that the parts I find difficult others may not. The prayer of humble access in *Common Worship* is a good example. This is the version I recall from childhood and the lack of worth always seemed to outweigh the mercy of God in my mind:

> We do not presume
> to come to this thy table, O merciful Lord,
> trusting in our own righteousness,
> but in thy manifold and great mercies.

We are not worthy
so much as to gather up the crumbs under thy table.
But thou art the same Lord
whose nature is always to have mercy.
Grant us therefore, gracious Lord,
so to eat the flesh of thy dear Son Jesus Christ
and to drink his blood,
that our sinful bodies may be made clean by his body
and our souls washed through his most precious blood,
and that we may evermore dwell in him, and he in us.
Amen.
(Holy Communion, Order One, in traditional language)

I do not ask people to say this prayer when I preside because in many instances I think that people feel unworthy enough without repeating it. However, Peter sees it very differently;

There is something beautiful for me about the timeless words which don't ask me to do something (forgive others), but rather state who I am – a sinner. The prayer of humble access is about me being a sinner before God. It isn't about shame for me but about ontological nature before a holy God. This prayer doesn't ask me to do anything which I can't do. Rather it welcomes me into God's presence and allows me to be washed clean – a sense of healing which I desperately need and want, and points me to eternity in his presence where all this worldly pain will be washed away. I need that!

Interestingly, for Peter it is the Lord's prayer that is difficult because it requires action, it expects him to do things he does not feel able to do at that point in time – forgive another. I don't think leaving out the Lord's prayer is an option in much of what I do but I need to be mindful of the consequences of expecting people to pray something they may not feel able to fully engage with or feel hypocritical in saying it, something that can lead us to experience shame.

Confession and absolution

The way most liturgical confessions are written is very guilt-focused: they are about what we have done or left undone. We need to consider confessing our shame too as that can also be a barrier to our ongoing discipleship and Christian journey. With shame we need to confess other things such as 'hiding from opportunities and failures in self-realization' (Pembroke 2010, pp. 41–3) but also could benefit from a liturgy of affirmation as well. Thus, a more holistic approach to confession and absolution may contain both forgiveness and affirmation. This prayer from Sandra Jebb is an example of this approach:

> God of grace and goodness, your mercy comes to us in ways that continually surprise us. You offer your mercy with no strings attached when we come to you with hearts ready and open. Forgive us those times when we focus on ourselves, and lack faith in your strength, love, and willingness to help us. Forgive us when we block out your call to take up new challenges, because we believe we're not able or equipped to do them. Forgive us when fear makes us small, and doubt invades our hopefulness; when we make all sorts of excuses, and try to hide from your loving gaze. Loving God, in our busy daily schedules from sunrise to sunset remind us again of your loving presence hovering near us and in us. Free us from the shame, self-doubt, and lack of faith that hinder us in the moment by moment possibilities that you set before us. Breathe your Spirit afresh on us so that we may be empowered to live in freedom, to act courageously, and to be active and fearless bearers of healing and mercy. We ask this through your Son Jesus, who touched and healed all who came to him. Amen. (Cited in Pembroke 2010, p. 14)

It might be that a variety of media could be used to mediate God's love, grace, mercy and forgiveness as well as verbal prayers. I remember as a young adult the power of listening to Graham Kendrick's (1974) song 'How much do you think you are worth?' which helped me to see myself more positively and addressed an identity based on shame and low self-esteem.

As an Anglican priest I normally use *Common Worship* (2000) but, as Daniel observes, *'we have fourteen of the fifteen Absolutions in Common Worship being precatory, depending on the minister asking for forgiveness and eleven of these start with the word 'May' making it sound as if God may or may not forgive'*. He goes on to argue that for those who are experiencing shame a more direct approach to absolution can be useful, thus, instead of the default absolution in *Common Worship* he suggests: *Almighty God, who forgives all who truly repent, has mercy upon you, pardons and delivers you from all your sins, confirms and strengthens you in all goodness, and keeps you in life eternal; through Jesus Christ our Lord.*

Gazing on the face of Christ

A common response to shame is to hide or cover our face but rather than do this we might benefit from gazing on the face of Jesus, the *visio dei* (Pattison 2013). One of my spiritual practices is to regularly visit the Chapel of the Blessed Sacrament at Buckfast Abbey in Devon and gaze upon the face of Christ in the form of a stained glass window; it is a healing experience for me because I feel loved by Jesus. I am not alone in this practice; several authors on shame recommend gazing upon Christ's face (Goodliff 2005, Pattison 2013, Pembroke 2010, Stockitt 2012). As Goodliff writes: 'Instead of hiding my face in shame, God wants me to look into his face with confidence in his acceptance and love for his care' (2005, p. 107). In a similar vein Stockitt argues that 'the mutuality of Christ gazing upon us in love and us reciprocating that gaze is an image of redemption and restoration' (2012, p. 153). There are many images of Christ that can be used in this way from a diversity of theological and cultural perspectives.

Forgiveness, repentance and restoration

For some, confession, repentance and forgiveness are part of responding to shame: *'Priests are God's ministers and have a duty – as we all do – not to overlook wrongdoing or to lead someone to believe they have not sinned when they have. They also have a duty to do so sometimes sensitively or very directly as the situation demands.'* Others preferred to emphasise the importance of the conviction of the Holy Spirit drawing someone towards repentance and working with them in a way that was felt to be in God's timing. Forgiveness is clearly associated with guilt, and thus, often about what we have done or not done, but there are elements of shame where it is important to forgive oneself or others and this can be a slow process.

Intercessions

Again, the most usual Anglican response in intercessions can be unhelpful for those who experience shame. 'Lord in your mercy, hear our prayer' can sound like we are pleading with God to listen to us and, for some, thinking that God will not is a default response. However, reading the Psalms shows how David had assurance of God listening to him:

> But truly God has listened;
> He has given heed to the words of my prayer.
> (Psalm 66.19)

Daniel paints this vivid picture:

> *I cringe regularly about how we miss the opportunity to enable a confident approach to God in prayer, enabling people to imagine 'Our Father' bending forward to hear everything from eloquence, to babble and groans that words cannot express . . . A simple change to the more affirming 'thank you for hearing/accepting our prayers' (even keeping the original versicle, 'Lord in your mercy . . .') enables*

an approach to God's throne with freedom and confidence. In the meantime, I have a picture of Jesus' wounded hands stretched out to all those saying or singing 'hear our prayer' with Jesus desperately crying out to them, 'but I do!'

Sharing the peace

In many contexts this involves greeting other people in the congregation in the prescribed way. This is difficult for some and can evoke shame or other difficult emotions for a variety of reasons. I was always conscious, for example, of not wanting to appear racist so I (not being a huggy person) was more likely to hug someone from a different ethnic background to me. I can overthink situations and find the peace easiest in small congregations when I can ensure I greet everyone. Making eye contact is important in communicating acceptance and is one of the first ways we bond as humans. Think how many times there is no eye contact when sharing the peace and what that may communicate to shame-prone people. Also consider how enforced contact, even just a handshake or in some contexts a hug or kiss can feel to a visitor or someone who has strong personal boundaries around physical touch.

Sung worship

Choosing what to sing in worship can be quite challenging. Given that for some people this might be one of their most significant engagements with theology we do well to consider what it is we are communicating. There are debates about such things as language and whether we change words in songs to make them more inclusive; about what atonement theology a song represents; whether songs are too romantic in nature – and much more. This is Peter's experience from his tradition:

In the more charismatic churches we sing songs about how good God is and how wonderful everything is. The words are generally twee and 'uplifting'. They are not uplifting

> *though. They again are crushing. This picture of a wonderful life filled with blessings only serves to highlight how painful 20 years of abuse are. My failings and my falling apart are then symptomatic of clearly having been a long way from God, because if I had been close to God then these things wouldn't have happened, would they? God is the good Father . . . so if I'm picking around in the pig sty for scraps to eat then it must have been me who ran away? Shame is very close at hand the more victorious the song seems to be.*

While I am not suggesting that we choose only from an approved list, we need to be aware that what we choose may impact people in a different way to how we imagine and might also want to consider if our teaching needs to counter any unhelpful theology which may be implicit in songs.

Preaching and teaching

I have rarely heard preaching or teaching on shame in the many years I have been going to church. Some of the messages that may be helpful to hear include making it clear we live in an imperfect world; we all make mistakes; Jesus doesn't see any sin as greater than another as reflected in the people he forgave; Jesus died a death of shame on the cross; justification by grace; focusing on loving God and loving others as the thing that Jesus said was most important rather than conforming to church cultural norms. As McNish makes clear, 'Jesus' birth, his ministry, his death, and his resurrection give us a paradigmatic model of shame transformed and resurrected' (2004, pp. 203–4). The story of Zacchaeus (Luke 19.1–10) is one often mentioned as the way Jesus engaged with someone experiencing shame, but I rarely hear the shame dimension mentioned.

Exploring shame positively

Worship, liturgy and ritual can be very positive experiences for people processing shame, but they may also be unhelpful and exacerbate the shame. Activities suggested here have been recommended by a range of people and I would encourage contextualization for your own context.

Child-friendly prayers

My shame experiences started when I was young and I didn't always feel that God accepted me as I was. Therefore, I think it is helpful if we can use prayers with children which help them understand God's love. These two prayers were written for the book by children's author Gemma Willis.

> When they tell me I'm not good enough
> **I am more, because you say I am**
> When they tell me I'll never make it
> **I am more, because you say I am**
> When they tell me I'm unwanted
> **I am more, because you say I am**
> When they tell me I'm dirty and worthless
> **I am more, because you say I am**
> **Help me Jesus, to see everyone as you see them, to be a bringer of worth, value and peace to those you love. Amen.**

> Thank you Jesus for showing me how valuable I am. Help me to show others how valuable they are too. I'm sorry for when I've made people feel unimportant or unwanted, thank you for loving me, no matter what. Help me to be all that you made me to be. Amen.

Writing a ritual

This is an example of a carefully crafted piece of ritual for a specific context but it can serve as a starting point for a range of issues. It was shared with me on the condition of anonymity of the authors. F = facilitator, P = participant and B = both or group if a corporate exercise. A = action, R = reading. Equipment: knotted ribbons

A liturgy of ending and of invitation into a new story: letting go of shame being wrapped in joy

F You are welcome in this place on this day, as we make this ending and mark this new beginning.

F A childhood of rejection, isolation, and loneliness, shame.

B **We acknowledge the tears, the pain, the panic, the shame.**
This was the old story, a part of my life but not all of my life.

F A childhood of grief, of loss, and sadness
A teenage life of grief and loss
The loss of a child, and all the hopes, and dreams, and love.

B **We acknowledge . . . the sorrow . . .**
This was the old story, a part of my life but not all of my life.

F A childhood of abuse, of anger, mismanagement, and of pain
A teenage life of bullying, of abuse and of injustice
An adult life with moments of terrible spiritual abuse.

B **We acknowledge . . . the injustice . . . abuse . . . the anger . . .**
This was the old story, a part of my life but not all of my life.

(This could be repeated as you needed and focused on parts of your story where there has been wounding or sorrow.)

P Changing it, warping it, stealing it,
Changing you, warping you, stealing you,
Changing it, warping it, stealing it,

B **This is the old story.**

A *(Undo the knotted ribbons, as a symbol of the knotted life, showing that the packaged-away grief and loss and shame of the old story has been undone. As this happens the following prayer is prayed . . .)*
Purple pain, bruised soul
Tears, Pain, Hurt, Anger
It is not fair:
It is so not fair

God – where on earth were you?
The why echoes – it feels purple
Be here now, God. I know you were there then.
As the knots unravel, feel the parts empty, fill them with your grace, your love, your light
I give you my shame, and leave it with you, Lord.
Help me be free.

F And now we join together to proclaim in God's presence the new story,
a story of welcome, of invitation, of being delighted in,
a story of growing, and thriving, and abundant life.

Proclaiming the truth

R (Choose as appropriate: Revelation 3.20; Isaiah 43.1–7; Isaiah 65.17–19 or a reading of choice. You may also want to read a story or poem which resonates, such as the shedding of Christian's burden in *Pilgrim's Progress.*)

A The un-knotted ribbons are now woven together/plaited together to symbolize the integration and weaving in of the old story transformed as part of the new story.

Reclaiming, Claiming, Proclaiming

F I name you as a child of God, a beloved daughter, a gifted and creative woman.
I name you as a loving wife and mother, who has not handed on the bitterness to the next generation, and who has not changed, stolen, warped the gifts and talents you have given to her daughters. We delight in them, and in all they are doing and daring. We ask you to bless them.
Now we set you free to live into your new story, taking with you and rejoicing in all that is good, allowing God to continue to heal and to work in your heart and life.

A (Anoint with oil, proclaiming freedom from shame, and/or put on a scarf, cloak or some other item of clothing that suggests God's covering the shame.)

Go in peace to love and serve the Lord
In the name of Christ. Amen.

Stations/actions

Many people find it helpful to engage in activities to help them process experiences. These have been shared with me by John and Olive Drane who have used them in creating a healing space in relation to shame. They recommend using them in the order below:

1 ***Dealing with hard stuff***
Equipment: tree branch/wood, big nails, hammer

Instruction sheet version 1
Our longings are sometimes too deep for words (Romans 8.26). Hammer a nail into the tree for those prayers you don't have the words to express.

Instruction sheet version 2
Just too hard to find words for . . .
Sometimes things are just like that – you can't find words to express yourself.
Maybe because you are facing circumstances that are just too hard to grapple with.
Or the old familiar words just don't cut it anymore.
Or well, . . . you're just fed up with talking all the time.

Romans 8.26 The Message.
Matthew 6.8.
Hammer a nail in here, take your time. Listen to each hammer blow.
Know that God knows the most incoherent of our prayers.

2 ***You are stained no more***
Equipment: large cross-shaped sheets of paper or cloth, disposable gloves, different coloured paint for hand prints, container for dirty gloves.

Instruction sheet
Reflect on what it is that is troubling you. Put on a glove and dip it into whichever colour speaks to you and then make a print or prints in any way you like. When you have done this, still wearing the glove, go to one of the leaders.

Leader's instructions
When someone comes to you, remove the messy glove and put it into a suitable container. Pray a blessing – as appropriate, but containing the phrase 'you are stained no more'.

3 ***Cleansing***
Equipment: Bowl of water and towel

Instruction sheet
Cleansing:
Without water, there is no life.
Every person in the UK uses 150 litres of water a day.
For 61 million people, that's a lot of water, more than 9 billion litres in fact. More than you can even imagine.
A third of all domestic water goes down the toilet.
A running tap wastes 10 litres of water every minute.
A dripping tap wastes 25 litres of water a day.
Take time to wash your hands. Be aware of the precious resource you are using. Think of all other parts of your life that you would like to be washed clean.
Maybe help another person by washing their hands, and talking about your needs for cleansing in all areas of life and relationships.

In the beginning, O God, your Spirit swept over the chaotic deep like a wild wind and creation was born.
In the turbulence of my own life and the unsettled waters of the world today let there be new birthing of your Spirit.
In the currents of my own heart and the upheaval of the world today let there be new birthing of your mighty Spirit.

Such activities may be part of a service of worship as well as other sorts of events. John tells a story of the power of water for cleansing as part of a service:

> Olive preached a sermon connecting with the pouring out of water at the Feast of Tabernacles, and we then invited people to do whatever they wished with water. One woman came to me and insisted on being soaked from head to foot, over her clothes and everything, telling me a horrific story of abuse and struggles with shame more or less from childhood. That was a couple of years ago and when I saw her again more recently she said that her life had completely turned around as a result.

Contemplative practices

Research suggests that centring prayer, resting in a loving God, may lead to a release of emotional wounds (Ferguson et al. 2010, p. 305). This is based on the model of Thomas Keating and suggest there are four moments:

- a sacred word (beginning of the prayer);
- rest (sense of God's Presence, Peace, Interior Silence);
- unloading (as a result of the deep rest of body, mind and spirit, the defence-mechanisms relax and the undigested emotional material of early life emerges from the unconscious at times in the form of a bombardment of thoughts of primitive emotions);
- evacuation (or primitive emotions and thoughts and return to sacred words)

(Ferguson et al. 2010, p. 311)

However, it is important not to feel shame when difficult thoughts emerge during the process as this is quite usual and does not mean we are not doing it right. For those trying new practices, being honest about how they might be experienced is helpful.

Storytelling

Telling stories can be an important tool in exploring shame as they encourage a fresh perspective. Testimony is a particular sort of storytelling that has a long history in the church, and that can be both liberating and community building. It can be helpful to encourage people 'not to be ashamed of their experiences, but to share their experiences in the hope and knowledge that their stories will be received by an encouraging community, and will also serve as encouragement for others' (Wright 2008, p. 195). While not all shame experiences may be appropriate to share in this way it can be encouraging to hear someone publicly speak about something we may be experiencing ourselves.

Alternatively, a retelling of biblical stories may be helpful, particularly when done in the first person as this can help a connection to our own story and enable us to get a fresh insight into God's perspective. Here are two examples from Nigel Roberts:

Salome

I wasn't proud of what I'd done. I was deeply ashamed. I'd been used. My mother used me. She made me . . . dance for Herod. And when I was done he was so filled with desire for me that he promised me anything. So I asked for the one thing I knew would kill him to give me – the head of John the Baptist. It was all my mother's idea. She hated the man, he was beginning to change things that my mother didn't want changed. So I asked for his head and got it. How strange that I now stand at the grave of the very man he preached about. Jesus. The very man my mother thought would turn the world upside down. And he has. My world at least. You see I've turned my back on everything I've done and everything I am and committed my life to following him. And he has accepted me; the killer of his cousin, the daughter of his enemy, without question and with love.

But they killed him. Pontius Pilate and my father together they crucified him. So now I follow him to the grave. I have nowhere else to go.

She stops and stares and turns. But it's empty.

The woman caught in adultery

I was in a dark place. I was on my knees and I couldn't look up. Around me a forest of legs and hands and in every hand a stone. If I had looked there would've been stone in every heart and a flint in every eye. The fingers were twitching on their rocks. Any moment now they would let them go and if I was lucky one would knock me out before the many took my life. It is a cruel and vicious way to die for what I've done. A high price for shame. I was scrabbling in the dirt trying to build a wall of mud around my body. Trying to hide my nakedness. My shame. A pathetic wall that could never save me; that would fall at the caress of the first pebble. And then a noise as a figure broke through the forest of legs and scrambled down the shale and knelt in front of me. He formed a wall of flesh and bone. He looked me in the eye and it was free of flint and full of love. Then he turned his gaze upon the crowd and I knew that I was saved, that I could once more stand tall and walk away.

Ignatian-style imaginative contemplation may also be helpful for some. The website Pray As You Go has a wide range (https://pray-as-you-go.org/article/imaginative-contemplation-exercises).

Wondering questions

If using Bible stories, Godly Play-style wondering questions may be a helpful tool to use as asking direct questions about shame can be pastorally inappropriate, even evoking more shame. The founder of Godly Play, Jerome Berryman, suggests that 'Wondering opens the creative process and draws both the lesson and . . . life experience into the personal creation of meaning' (2009, p. 45) and this meaning often relates to identity. Some of the questions that may be used (in relation to Bible stories) include:

- I wonder which part of this story you like best? *This supports disclosure of feelings.*
- I wonder what part of the story is the most important? *This encourages thinking.*
- I wonder where you are in the story? I wonder what part is about you? *This invites personal involvement.*
- I wonder if there is any part of the story we can leave out and still have all the story we need? *This encourages reflection and critique.*

(Berryman 2009, pp. 49–50)

With shame I have always believed that I need to explore my own life to enable me to journey alongside others and so I reflected on the story of the woman at the well (John 4.4–26; see Nash 2016 for a fuller discussion of my understanding of this approach):

- ***I wonder which part of this story you like best?***
  I like the part where Jesus sat down by a well because he was tired. I don't always find it easy to rest, particularly in 'work hours' although I know I do more hours than might be expected. That Jesus felt tired helps me to see that he was fully human and that if I gave him a chance to talk to me he might well say, Sally, come and sit down and join me by this well. We can have a drink and relax together. I find myself finding it hard to justify self-care choices sometimes while encouraging them in others. Somewhere there is still a sense of shame in not getting everything done that needs to be done. I am not a good Centre Director, priest, daughter, wife etc. if I have not . . .

- ***I wonder what part of the story is the most important?***
  The most important part of the story is where the woman responds positively to Jesus and asks him for the living water, she wants to receive what it is that Jesus has to offer. She is receiving from someone who first asked her to give to him, there was a mutuality of sharing even though a differential in what was given.
- ***I wonder where you are in the story? I wonder what part is about you?***
  I am the woman, the person with the baggage and history that sometimes holds her back. My baggage is different to hers, but there are times when I try to hide a bit or avoid situations or see myself in her at the beginning of the story rather than the full of joy messenger of good news at the end of the story.
- ***I wonder if there is any part of the story we can leave out and still have all the story we need?***
  I don't think we need to know what it is that she has done wrong in the past, perhaps just that she has done something wrong but that Jesus talks to her and sets her free.

If I were to follow the usual pattern of a Godly Play story I would then make a creative response. Mine might be a picture of Jesus sitting on top of a pile of my baggage that he has taken from me. I have purposefully chosen to answer the questions in ways which are comfortable for me given they are in the public domain; in a more private context I might have answered them differently depending on how safe I felt or what aspects of my experience I felt might resonate with who I was talking to.

Theological statements

Inherent within much liturgy are theological statements which we are encouraged to say. Another resource to use with those who are shamed are theological statements which seek to address the shame more overtly than many do. Nelson (2016,

p. 31) identifies what Jesus does in relation to shame, and these words could be spoken over someone or spoken in the first person:

- Jesus comes to give honour instead or dishonour – all the ways you have felt and experienced rejection.
- Jesus clothes you with beauty, removing the ashes of shame you've worn for your sin or for the sinful atrocities committed against you.
- He comforts you as you mourn, releasing you from the shame of grieving alone or without purpose.
- Whether in this life or in the one to come, he brings justice for the injustice you've suffered because of your race, faith, gender, or family.
- Jesus brings favour – oh, favour of the Lord that is permanent and unchanging – instead of the vague cloud of constant approval.

The following is a theological prayer, written by Scotty Smith, which could be printed and given to people to pray to seek to internalize a different perspective on their shame:

> *And the man and his wife were both naked and felt no shame.* Genesis 2.25
>
> Gracious Father, it's nearly impossible for me to imagine the day when there was no need for the emotion of shame. In their innocence, our first parents were absolutely free of any need to turn away from your gaze, or that of one another.
>
> There was nothing to fear or cover up; no need to hide, pose, or pretend; nothing to get defensive or feel guilty about; no need to make excuses or blame the other; no attempt to disappear, do penance, medicate, or try any other broken attempt to deal with the disintegrating effects of shame. What a blessed state of affairs, all lost because of sin.
>
> It is only in you, Lord Jesus, that we now find hope to deal with both our guilt and our shame. For in light of the joy set

before you by the Father, you endured the agony of the cross for us, scorning its shame—the shame of being made sin for us, that in you we might become the righteousness of God (Hebrews 12.2; 2 Corinthians 5.21).

Indeed, Jesus, those who trust in you will never be put to shame, for you took our shame and made it yours (1 Peter 2.6); as a result, we now live in the present delight and eternal favor of God. O, even more blessed state of affairs. How can we ever praise you enough for such love?

Therefore, Jesus, we cry out for freedom today – freedom in our ongoing struggles with shame, both the shame we feel and the shame we give. Though our guilt has been completely taken care of by your work on the cross, Jesus, we still feel varying degrees of shame, and we act out in a variety of destructive ways.

We vacillate between self-contempt and other-centered contempt; both of these contradict and sabotage the very love by which, and for which, we were saved. Forgive us when, out of fear, anger and pride, we shame others – especially those closest to us. Indeed, we need the freedom you alone can provide, Jesus. Bring the grace and truth of the gospel to bear in profoundly healing and liberating ways, Lord Jesus.

We praise you that as this day begins, we are fully and eternally accepted in you. The gospel is true, beautiful and powerful. So very Amen we pray, in your merciful and mighty name.

(www.thegospelcoalition.org/blogs/scotty-smith/a-prayer-about-shame-its-effects-and-resolve/)

Creative writing

Finally, pieces of creative writing can make connections with people who find more traditional elements of liturgy unhelpful and they can also evoke recognition in us because we are hearing the words afresh rather than the familiarity of an often read

Bible story. They also serve as examples for creative writing to inspire others to write themselves and process some of their shame. Here are some examples (the first two are based on biblical passages):

The poor in spirit

Blessed are the poor in spirit,
Those who feel they're not enough
Those whose lives feel tough,
Who struggle sometimes just to keep on going.
Blessed are the weak,
The wobbly, the insecure
Those who feel uncertain or unsure.
Blessed are those who doubt,
who question, wonder,
Shout frustration up to heaven.

Blessed are those who struggle to forgive
Others and themselves.
Who want to live as God would have them live
But feel sometimes they just can't face the day.
Blessed are those who pray
and though feeling the imperfection of their prayers
keep praying anyway.

Blessed are those who sigh
Who try but fear they try in vain
Blessed are those in pain,
Those whose Sunday smiles hide broken hearts
Whose dreams seem shattered on the ground
Those who carry childhood hurts around.
Blessed are those who make mistakes
Those who feel they don't have what it takes
Those who have slipped up, messed up
Have missed it, blown it, are past it.

Blessed are those who feel they just don't fit
Those who find themselves
On the edge or in the shade.

Blessed those who feel their Christian lives
Don't make the grade.
Blessed those who long to pray more,
Worship more, understand more.
Blessed are the poor in spirit.

(Jo Whitehead)

Shame

You search me and know me,
You know when I sit and when I rise; you perceive my thoughts from afar.
You discern my going out and my lying down; you are familiar with all my ways.
There are many parts of my story that I race past,
holding my breath lest they raise their heads and show me up for who I fear I am.
Small things that grow from my hidden corners, swelling, filling, misshaping me.
Things I am told, looks that I catch in the eyes of another.
The leaping of my heart as heat rises and dizziness flows.
They grow and overwhelm, forcing me back into their dark places.
Deep into my shame I have sunk.
You search me and know me,
You know when I sit and when I rise; you perceive my thoughts from afar.
You discern my going out and my lying down; you are familiar with all my ways.
In the night my spirit wakes and taunts me,

The voices that tell me I can do no good, that I have no value,
That remind me of my failings, of my weakness, of my splinters and shards.
The faces that stare with eyes which condemn and dismiss me,
That look with disdain and judgement, that puncture my faith.
The sneers and comparisons, the taunts and the jokes.
Deep into my shame I have shrunk.
You search me and know me,
You know when I sit and when I rise; you perceive my thoughts from afar.
You discern my going out and my lying down; you are familiar with all my ways.
In the morning I face myself in the mirror and see what I have done.
My past actions overwhelm me and change what I see,
They tell me I am wicked, they tell me I am ugly,
They drown my goodness, they suffocate my beauty.
They fight to own and define me, and too often they win.
They become who I am and what I may be.
Deep into my shame I have grown.
Where can I go from your Spirit?
Where can I flee from your presence?
If I go up to the heavens, you are there;
if I make my bed in the depths, you are there.
If I rise on the wings of the dawn,
if I settle on the far side of the sea,
even there your hand will guide me,
your right hand will hold me fast.
If I say, 'Surely the darkness will hide me and the light become night around me',
even the darkness will not be dark to you;
the night will shine like the day,
for darkness is as light to you.
Your eyes search me,

You know my heart.
See through my shame,
See deep into my hidden places,
See through my deepest fear and pain,
Show me what you see,
Show me the me you created,
Show me the goodness you know is there,
Show me the strength I cannot feel,
Show me the beauty I cannot see,
Show me the light in my darkness,
Show me the music in my soul.
Help me to release the things I have done that I have let define me,
Help me to release the things that others have done to me that crush my spirit,
Help me to know the difference I make for others,
Help me to trust the difference you make in me,
Help me to be the me you see,
Help me to be the me you love,
Help me to recognize myself in you.
For you created my inmost being;
you knit me together in my mother's womb.
I praise you because I am fearfully and wonderfully made;
your works are wonderful, I know that full well.
Mother and Father God,
Creator, Redeemer, Comforter,
Search me, know me, love me,
Help me to search myself,
Help me to know myself,
Help me to love myself.
Forgive me for the things I have done that shame me,
Forgive me for the things I regret not doing,
Forgive me for not trusting in your grace and love.
Help me to accept total forgiveness,
Help me to live from this day without guilt or shame,
Help me to trust in your grace and love,
Lead me forward in peace and new life.

Search me, God, and know my heart;
test me and know my anxious thoughts.
See if there is any offensive way in me,
and lead me in the way everlasting.

Mark Berry (Extracts from Psalm 139 NIV)

Fitting in

Square peg, round hole.
I attempt to mould myself to shape,
only to revert,
and have to try again to fit.
So, I wonder about giving up.
Unlearning all that I have learned to conform,
and maybe stand out instead.
Yes, today
I dropped the mask
as I once again tripped.
But no grief.
I think I learned instead
that growth might be mispresented.
That true gain may be in the releasing of pretence.
The safe definition
and distracting finery
to disguise our differences,
what need do we have of these?
Yes, I wonder about
shedding the trappings of success,
stored for false assurance.
And instead, undressing,
stepping out and owning
the full sum of my truth.
Square peg, round hole.

Humility, that hard honest lesson,
has a welcome voice,
'Accept yourself,' it says.
'Allow shame to fall.'

(Ana Lisa de Jong, https://livingtreepoetry.com/)

Deeper than words go

Deeper than words go,
well below
the summer sun's
warming glow
and the scalpel's reach,
wounds graffiti the human soul.
Old abandoned wounds,
overgrown, derelict, dark,
littered with decaying damp detritus.
Sparkly new wounds,
grand designs
glistening with fresh, pungent paint;
landscaped to perfection.
The wounds of human shame
that outlast old age, sore as hell,
seeping,
  weeping,
    leaking pain,
poisoning the soul's resistance
to the shadows of the past.

(Tim Sumpter)

All sorts of creativity may be helpful to process shame and the examples in this chapter will hopefully inspire a wide range of other ideas.

Reflection questions

- Are there aspects of the liturgy that you find challenging in relation to shame?
- Is there a Bible story that you find helpful in relation to shame? What would your answers to the wondering questions be?
- Which material from this chapter could you try out in practice?
- Are you working with anyone who would find creative writing a helpful way to help them process their shame? How can you facilitate this?
- Have you identified any changes you want to make in your praxis in the light of this chapter?

7

Pastoral Care with Those Experiencing Shame

Introduction

> There is a wonderful example and paradigm for the overcoming of shame and alienation. Jesus looks up into Zacchaeus's face from below, thus, being anything but invasive, bullying, or dominating. He calls Zacchaeus by name, showing respect for him. He then asks something of Zacchaeus that he can easily give, demonstrating that he does not despise or reject him and affirming his efficacy and agency. The recognition of personhood and inclusion and affirmation that Jesus offers makes Zacchaeus want to include himself further. (Pattison 2011, p. 27)

This is an example of how Jesus approaches someone who is likely to be shamed in his cultural context. In essence, Jesus honours Zacchaeus in the encounter. That begins to give a glimpse of some of the qualities and practices we need to demonstrate in engaging with those who are experiencing shame. In John 20.20–29 Peter, along with the other disciples, is commissioned by Jesus but in chapter 21 we find him back fishing and it is only after a further intervention from Jesus (21.15–19) that addressed his shame that he continues in what God has called him to. This is a reminder that as we think about pastoral care with those who experience shame we need to make sure that we have engaged with our own. It is also helpful when thinking about pastoral care to be reminded again that

> We avoid and fear shame maybe even more than we avoid suffering. Shame strips us of our defences against our fragile mortality. We have no justice to call on, no public esteem to hope for, no leg to stand on. Just feel that blush that engulfs your whole body. Shame is nakedness in the face of ridicule, vulnerability in the face of blame, and guilt without excuse. If wisdom is going to speak from the depths, it must pierce our pride and reach our shame. (Wells 2013, p. xviii)

Shame occurs across the life cycle and there are, as we have seen in previous chapters, many triggers for it. Some of the most common we may want to look out for are:

- Infancy and young childhood: shame and mortification of complete powerlessness;
- Adolescence: developing body and unruly manifestation of sexuality;
- Adulthood: not being or having what you hoped or expected; losses, abandonments and rejections by love objects; failures of every kind;
- Older: decline of physical and mental powers, sexual prowess, physical attractiveness, youthful appearance.

(McNish 2003, p. 7)

It is also the case that pastoral carers do not always distinguish well between guilt and shame and the way people are 'counselled toward confession and forgiveness, which are appropriate responses to guilt but premature or ineffective responses to shame' (Thomas and Parker 2004, p. 176). This chapter seeks to suggest ways in caring for people experiencing shame.

One of the important dimensions of pastoral care is to help those we are accompanying to identify if the experience of shame is ours or if it has been imposed by others inappropriately. Sometimes we may need to help people to see that some of the shame they are experiencing is not theirs but that they have picked up on the negative attitudes and views of others.

It may also be that being part of the church is exacerbating shame from a different part of their life.

Engendering confidence

One of my findings was that for some, their capacity to share their shame with a pastoral carer was related to how that person presented themselves. If leaders are authentic about who they are and their own struggles and failures (within the constraint of those still enabling those they lead to feel safe), this makes them more approachable and facilitates building high quality relationships. Jackie said: *'I personally would quite like it if my church leader was vulnerable and was open about their failings. I would relate and say, we're all in the same boat. Let's come and work this through together.'* Looking at how to build trust and being aware of what destroys trust is important when working with people experiencing shame. Often they are hoping to be able to be themselves at church rather than put on a mask or carefully guard their words. This means that one of the things we can consider is purposefully developing our pastoral care skills. 'The really gifted and graced helper knows, however, that when she allows herself to enter heart and soul into the relationship, it is not so much words or techniques which are healing and renewing but her very presence' (Pembroke 2002, p. 75).

Referral

It is vital to note that there will be some instances of shame which are beyond our capacity: *'It's important to recognize my own limitations to the help I can offer, otherwise, the person may suffer more shame.'* Thus, referring someone on to professional counselling or to someone with more expertise in this area should always be considered. However, continuing to support the person can be important as they may feel more shame if they feel they have just been passed on because they are too difficult or feel rejected because you now do not engage with them any more. There is no shame for us in needing to do this.

Raising issues that may cause shame

High quality relationships made it easier to raise issues without an individual experiencing shame, although some individuals are more shame-prone than others. Paula observed that *'if we feel accepted unconditionally by someone then them saying to you that's not really the best way of doing things – that's the wrong way of doing things – doesn't make you feel ashamed.'* Simon commented that *'sometimes the church is so passive aggressive that we don't know what to do when somebody actually looks us in the eye and says "Do you know what? That was wrong. You've behaved really badly there".'* In both these examples guilt ('I have done something wrong') may be the appropriate response but the danger is it moves into shame ('there is something wrong with me'), particularly if addressed with lack of sensitivity and skill. This may involve identifying the most appropriate person to raise an issue or establishing a culture of mutual accountability. Hearing about a leader of a national mission organization apologizing to the staff for some of their interpersonal interactions is a good example of how mutual accountability might begin to flourish which gives the possibility of appropriate challenge without shaming.

Naming and reframing

Research suggests that shame is not always easy to recognize until awareness is raised and, even then, sometimes it is difficult to acknowledge or own it. People also become skilled at hiding their shame:

> Hiding is our go-to coping skill to guard ourselves against the pain of disapproval or judgment, condemnation or mockery, belittlement or exposure, or worse – just fill in the blank with your unique circumstance. We put on masks of pretense, we erect protective shields around our hearts to deflect the shame or distract unwanted attention. Enough practice and we become masters at hiding from others and eventually

ourselves – and ultimately we hide from God, thinking that somehow, if we're not seeing him, then he must not be seeing us. (Caine 2016, p. 31)

Sometimes identifying and speaking out means that the hold something has on us reduces and we can begin a process of change. Acknowledging shame can help repair social bonds that are broken rather than exacerbating conflict through lack of acknowledgement (Scheff & Retzinger 2001). One area of reframing that may be necessary is perceptions of God who may be seen as punitive, loving conditionally or abandoning, for example. These views of God can come from childhood care or experiences and some of us can bury or ignore parts of ourselves that appear unacceptable in church (Catford 2010). Theological and biblical insights discussed in Chapter 2 may be helpful with this as well as some of the practices suggested below.

Creating a safe space

For an individual experiencing shame, creating a safe space where they can express themselves when they are ready is an important starting point. However, it is important not to rush people. One piece of guidance received was:

> *Don't try to 'say the right thing' too quickly as 'the right thing' has often been misused. Be clear and don't quote scripture at them to reassure them; and be very careful about offering to pray with someone until they know you better, this is often all misused in spiritual abuse, and however sincere you are, it will trigger them into freeze, fight or flight responses, and they may comply and act like they are ok about it but run away after and never come back.*

One dilemma is that for some people a church leader is not a safe person. This comment is illustrative of several: '*No I would not like to talk to a church leader because they are the leader and I would feel that they would always look at me in light of my revelations. I have no idea how someone could help me unless that person was someone I could confide in and trust to remain neutral about me. There is no-one in my church who fits this role.'* Communicating that this is not the case may be important, but this also needs to be true. This is in part a theological issue around how individuals are seen in the light of all being made in the image of God (Genesis 1.27) and of equal worth and not subject to a degrading label. In an educational setting I strive for space that is open, boundaried and hospitable (Palmer 1993) and these are useful concepts for considering in relation to ministry with those experiencing shame. It is another reason for having a clearly identifiable pastoral care team made up of a range of people – for historical reasons, not everyone can trust the clergy.

Listening

It almost seems too obvious to say that listening is the most important thing to do with people who have experienced shame, but it is the most frequently quoted response. This is a consistent theme in literature on pastoral practice also: 'Listening is that crucial act of love for which human beings long. With careful listening can come the gifts of being heard, known, understood' (Moschella 2008, p. 254). These are the skills seen as particularly important:

- taking time to gain trust;
- being non-judgemental;
- being empathetic;
- reflecting back as appropriate;
- taking note of verbal and non-verbal cues;
- helping people see they are not alone in feeling shame;
- discerning the core issues;
- validating the right to have a different perspective from others;
- identifying what spiritual and practical resources someone has;
- seeking to identify ways of processing shame in a healthy way.

Prayer and mediating how God sees an individual underpinned many people's approach. As one person noted: *'It's a very long term process, listening, listening and listening, identifying, trying to create a new pattern of behaviour.'* Connected to this is the importance of presence and the damage done if we are defective in our presence towards someone experiencing shame. This can reinforce rather than ameliorate it; availability may well be more important than skill in such relationships (Pembroke 2002). However, training is helpful to reduce the likelihood of inappropriate support being offered.

Acceptance, affirmation and assurance

Shame often occurs because of a defective relationship and that is so important to address. A recurring theme of my research was offering acceptance and affirmation along with an assurance of God's love. Responses on this theme included *'Love, love and more love. Mixed with acceptance and compassion as consistently as possible'* and *'Personally I would try and explain that God accepts you however you come. I would try and help by showing acceptance and care through my behaviour and attitudes towards that person.'* Other insights included:

- seeing the individual as a person not a problem;
- encouraging rather than condemning;
- helping people see the good in themselves;
- recognizing we have all fallen short – they are not alone;
- trying to help people to love themselves;
- understanding that someone may need to be sought out rather than expecting them to come to us;
- using holding and appropriate touch (within safeguarding guidelines), remembering that embodied responses are what work best for some people.

It may be helpful to note this observation: *'Most people don't need to be told they've done wrong, but pretending that they haven't doesn't help and makes us look dishonest.'* Clearly this comment only applies to some areas of shame and reassuring people that they were not at fault can be imperative in many instances.

Although the concepts sound straightforward it can be challenging to offer acceptance, affirmation and assurance. For example, establishing appropriate boundaries and realistic expectations may be necessary and have to be held in tension with loving acceptance. One insightful observation was about the value of recognizing that '*it may be difficult for someone to accept love and kindness and they may try to push it/me away, so it is important to see beyond any behaviour and let consistent warmth and acceptance do its work*'. For shame to be alleviated the acceptance and affirmation needs to be internalized.

Sometimes the presenting issue will not be the original source of the shame that is being experienced and a person may have become trapped in shame-based responses or have become particularly shame-prone. It may take some time to uncover the original trigger. Self-affirmation may also be a part of what is required but for this to happen it may be that the opportunity offered to receive affirmation and acceptance needs to be accessible and risk free.

Helping people to feel sufficient

This is a slight nuance from the previous section which emerged from the research and focuses on the importance of acknowledging our shared humanity and membership of the body of Christ. One useful insight was from Simon who emphasised the importance from his experience of '*offering and receiving respect, and being treated as an equal, not as an object in ministry*'. A similar statement was made: '*people who minister can sometimes be a right pain in the backside. I do not need ministry; I need love*'. 'Our task as pastors is to legitimize, validate and hold the shame experience of our people, to help them face it and surround it with a strengthened ego position within the context of trustworthy Christian community' (McNish 2003, p. 19). Sieff suggests that 'ultimately it is what we experience within the context of healing relationships that enables us to ameliorate shame' (2015, p. 233). Several church members responded about what they were looking for in a church leader when wanting to discuss shame. For example, '*There is nothing worse than turning to a higher authority in the church and still feeling judged by them when you are looking for support*', and '*God has no favourites – we all come to him from the same starting point and that is how we should see ourselves, including clergy.*' One person talked about the importance of helping people move from shame to anger and seeking justice in a situation where that was appropriate and possible. Another suggested that in his experience as a spiritual director shame was sometimes masking anger at the church or was a response to crass pastoral activity and facilitating people to see this was part of helping them process and move on from it. It was also important to try and encourage people to see that the feelings of insufficiency were unmerited.

Building community

This is the communal version of acceptance, affirmation and assurance and encourages an institutional capacity to engage with shame. One possibility is to explore the communal identity which is inherent in being part of the family of God, which for some may mean redeeming the concept of family. It is important to incorporate those experiencing shame into a '*loving community and through things like fun and hospitality help the person value themselves and explore their preconceptions of faith and God*'. There were other responses around inviting people to coffee, or meals, and generally trying to include them in things that happened in the church, helping them to find acceptance within a wider circle. One leader commented: '*I think a functioning community is the most important part of "my" ministry.*' Another person suggests that '*There is a need to be real with one another and open with each other. Too often the shame comes from what we feel others think. My experience is that when people get down to real conversations and build real relationships, love and acceptance are naturally demonstrated.'* What is integral to this is appropriate and effective communication patterns which contribute to building community. What may be important is to develop the 'carrying capacity' (Newbrough 1995, p. 24) of a community, which in more church-oriented language is perhaps what could be called a functioning body of Christ with every member ministry (1 Corinthians 12).

Self-perception and biblical perspectives

Challenging and changing negative self-perceptions is an element of supporting those who are experiencing shame. For some, using the Bible to help them see themselves and their shame as God sees them can be beneficial. That we are made in the image of God (Genesis 1.27) is a starting point:

> the image of God is a promise and an assurance that one's humanity is not determined by philosophical, theological, social or cultural constructs, but is held and sustained by the very hand of God as he reaches out to affirm the humanness of each person irrespective of their circumstances . . . the doctrine of the imago Dei is a deeply pastoral doctrine which offers hope to the hopeless, comfort to the downhearted and a wholeness to those whose lives have been broken and damaged by fate and circumstances. (Swinton 2000, p. 32)

Verses such as Philippians 2.5 'Let the same mind be in you that was in Christ Jesus', which implies wholeness and well-being, and Romans 12.2 'be transformed by the renewing of your minds' highlights the importance of the way we think; changing thought patterns is often important in shame. Remembering that through his death Jesus bore our shame can be helpful. Many Gospel stories may help people change their self-perception. The woman with the haemorrhage (Luke 8.43–8), and the woman caught in adultery (John 7.52–8.11) whom Jesus did not condemn, were the most frequently cited stories to help people understand the response of Jesus to shame. One person comments on the former story that it '*says a great deal about the pain, loneliness and desperation people can feel, Jesus embodies what the church should do in those situations. When a person filled with shame reaches out we should stop and engage with that person, talk to them and value them.*' Such stories are important because they '*show Jesus accepting individuals as they are in that moment, not condemning their past, or parading it before them and the onlookers. He shows great warmth and gentleness in acknowledging these people have a future*'. Examples where someone did something wrong but was then restored can also be helpful. The prodigal son (Luke 15.11–32) was suggested as illustrating the '*love of God in extreme measure*' and the shame and guilt felt by the son. The story of David and Uriah (2 Samuel 11.2–27) was offered as another example of God continuing to love us when we fall, restoring and working through us. The way Jesus responded to Peter's indiscretions (John 21.1–9) is another useful illustration. The choice of Mary as the mother of Jesus may provide hope to some: as someone commented, '*God has a purpose for us all, however small, scared or like a nobody we may feel. The shame Mary must have felt and the pain she went through but all for a meaning.*'

Creative media

If we understand creativity as part of what it means to be made in the image of God, then creative activities may open people up to God and their own potential (Ford 2011). Creativity also embraces the notion that formulaic ministry will not necessarily work as each person's experience of shame is different and they may respond to a variety of resources, rituals or symbols (Albers 1995). The use of art and literature in facilitating the exploration of 'problematic aspects of their personality, without undue anxiety' (Nussbaum 2004, p. 296) is one to be explored. Art journals are a tool that may be helpful in exploring emotions; Soneff talks about 'finding peace in the midst of emotional turmoil' (2008, p. 5) through using introspective journalling using a range of media in the context of a healing journal. Similarly, therapeutic journal writing may assist some people given its reflective and reflexive nature and may help someone find their own voice in relation to things that may have been 'previously unknown, unspeakable, or unacknowledged' (Thompson 2011, p. 31). It may also help in the identification of coping strategies. However, advocating such practices may need to be done with caution, with appropriate support and ideally with some personal experience of the discipline. Using creative activities alongside talking can also be useful as it gives a focus and means that continual eye contact is not always necessary, which is helpful with shame, although some eye contact is helpful to communicate acceptance and affirmation.

Drawing on appropriate resources

Resources that seem appropriate to support and help someone experiencing shame may partly depend on our spiritual tradition. Berry argues that she has 'become increasingly aware of the importance of imagery, symbol, and symbolic action as people work through the impact of significant, life-changing events in their own experience' (2009, p. 2). One person suggested allowing for *'the church's older practices like Lectio Divina and meditation to offer room for personal contemplation where the focus is on the individual's relationship with the divine rather than listening to a preacher pontificating about what is right'*. For some, very practical activities such as banging nails into a wooden cross or writing or drawing things and burning them can be helpful. There are also occasions where these sorts of processes need to be done corporately, not just individually. There is some evidence that spiritual practices can be helpful with difficult emotions such as shame. For example, centring prayer, resting in a loving God, may lead to a release of emotional wounds (Ferguson et al. 2010). As mentioned in the previous chapter, gazing upon the face of Christ can be significant in transforming our shame.

Wimberly (2011, pp. 81–2) offers the metaphor of a journey in moving beyond shame, and his list may be helpful to share or encourage someone to engage with:

- invite Jesus to journey with you;
- persevere, refuse to accept the shame, perceiving self as a sojourner on a journey where the future can be different;
- use spiritual practices to keep close to God, perceiving self as a child who is part of God's household cared for by Jesus;
- listen to, seek and rely on God to experience peace, rest and joy;
- connect with others on the same journey as well as stories of others who have journeyed before, worship, confess hope and know that overcoming shame is possible.

Finding an approach that resonates with an individual's spiritual tradition may make it easier for them to engage although this does not negate the idea of them trying something new which may give a fresh insight.

Forgiveness

Issues around forgiveness may emerge but are best engaged with when a person is ready. This may take a considerable time and meanwhile being affirming and loving is important. People who have experienced shame may well be sensitive to being treated as a 'case' where the aim is to close the case. Thus, one person talked about *'trying to make sure I avoid anything that would give the impression that I am avoiding them'*. Another insight was trying to ensure that the church doesn't add to their shame, which may require addressing issues or even people in the church if there is any inappropriate behaviour. To feel God's forgiveness we need acceptance from God's people; the capacity to internalize this forgiveness results in a more loving conscience (Cloud 1990).

A small number of people focused on the importance of confession, forgiveness and repentance as part of responding to shame. For example: *'Priests are God's ministers and have a duty – as we all do – not to overlook wrongdoing or to lead someone to believe they have not sinned when they have. They also have a duty to do so sometimes sensitively or very directly as the situation demands.'* However, some made it clear that this was only appropriate in contexts where the person concerned was experiencing the conviction of the Holy Spirit and was being drawn to repentance. Some framed this within an emphasis of God's grace, understanding that God knows and loves us while seeking to show empathy and understanding themselves. One person discussed the difference between healthy and unhealthy shame, the former bringing about repentance and restoration of relationship and the dangers of shame without hope and redemption. Forgiveness is clearly associated with guilt; with shame it is more complex but there are some elements of shame where one needs to forgive oneself or others, which may be a slow process (de Smet 2007).

Honouring

I have a growing awareness of the importance of honouring as a ministerial praxis toward individuals both one-to-one and in public, through social media as well as in teaching, church activities and so on. In honouring others, we are sharing the honour of Christ. It is one way of trying to provide a counterbalance against the shame people may be carrying although in and of itself it cannot redress the shame. This seems to be a key theme emerging from the research – that some shaming can be avoided if an attitude is adopted of consciously treating everyone with honour (Campbell 2003). I am particularly keen to honour those who work hard behind the scenes to make things happen. Those of us who have up-front ministries are honoured in different ways but we cannot do what we do without the work of so many others who serve faithfully week by week. I will often try to give examples when I preach; for example, 'the lovely Millie made a coffee cake for me to take down to my Mum, the wonderful Steve sets up the communion table for me knowing I like a stand so I can read the liturgy more easily'. I also try to affirm people on social media, partly by the adjectives I might use to describe them but also by expressing my gratitude for them and who they are. Commissioning different groups in church helps to honour the roles people take on and expressing, for example, that the coffee team are part of the hospitality and welcome team, can honour those whose contribution is just as vital but less obvious than those who may normally be given a higher profile.

Ministerial praxis

The God I believe in will determine how I understand the church, and both of these things impact ministerial praxis. What emerged from my research was that one of the most crucial tasks of ministerial praxis in relation to shame is to create an environment in which inappropriate shaming does not happen and where people feel safe to share their shame, if needed. An awareness that experiencing shame may increase self-sufficiency and reduce reliance on family and friends (Chao et al. 2011) suggests that we may need to be proactive in reaching out to those who may want to withdraw. Integral to this is an understanding of hospitality that creates a space 'where the dignity of every human person is vouchsafed, embraced, and protected, deep within the heart of the church' (Beck 2011, p. 140). The injunction of Jesus to 'love the Lord your God with all your heart, and with all your soul, and with all your strength, and with all your mind; and your neighbour as yourself" (Luke 10.27) is perhaps a good starting point for exploring how to set such a culture. However, experience suggests that it can require a proper understanding of what it means to love ourselves to fully appropriate this verse. This might include 'having integrity, taking care of yourself and being self-protective when it is required' (Layder 2004, p. 36). It could also include a resilience towards shame and the capacity to process shaming incidents in a way that does not leave a lasting legacy.

Skilled companionship

In some contexts, shame may be exacerbated because of perceptions of the relationship between the person offering pastoral care and the cared for. Thinking this through can be important in ministry. Although talking about nursing, Campbell's notion of 'skilled companionship' (1985, pp. 49–50) is one that resonates in my own ministry experience. He suggests that it encompasses 'closeness which is not sexually stereotyped; it implies movement and change; it expresses mutuality; and it requires commitment but within defined limits' (p. 49). This companionship involves bodily presence, helping a person move forward in their journey, a degree of mutuality inherent in being with rather than just doing to, and a limited commitment realizing that there are other dimensions to the life of the carer as well as often a time-limited relationship. What I particularly like about the use of the term 'companionship' is its echoes of the Eucharist, with the term deriving from an old French term *compaignon* which can be literally translated as 'one who breaks bread with another' (www.oxforddictionaries.com).

Addressing an issue at the right level

One of the insights I have found helpful in thinking about shame and what my approach to it should be comes from organizational thinking. I consider which of five levels a problem is impacting or needs to be addressed at:

- environment;
- behaviour;
- skills and abilities;
- beliefs and values;
- identity.

(Sartain and Katsarou 2011, pp. 110–11)

This helps me to explore the best strategy to approach the issue. While one-to-one pastoral work may often be necessary, sometimes the root cause needs addressing in a different dimension or from a broader perspective. I have found it helpful to think this through as sometimes simple changes in environment or behaviour can provide a solution to a problem, though at other times it is much more complex and attention needs to be given to articulating values and/or building consensus. This model also helps me identify where shame I may be experiencing could be coming from and to consider if any tweaks or adjustments are necessary.

Conclusion

In this chapter I have tried to highlight some of the practical things we need to do as we offer pastoral care to those who have been shamed. It will often be a long-term commitment and we may need to address issues at different levels. Helpfully, it is often listening that is the most important thing we can do and there are many in our churches who can and will do this well. We do well to remember that 'Shame feelings alert us to our failures in presence. The challenge is to find the courage and the commitment, under God, to change' (Pembroke 2002, p. 194). This is an example of how healthy shame in us may help us as we seek to support others in their shame. However, we do need to remember to offer appropriate support to those who are supporting others. There is often no point in trying to work with those who are experiencing shame without addressing those things that trigger or cause shame. The next two chapters explore this in more detail.

Reflection questions

- Does the story of Zacchaeus trigger any memories or part of yourself that causes you shame? How does Jesus' response in the story help you?

- Are you clear on the how and when of pastoral referrals in your context?
- What are your strengths and weaknesses as a listener?
- Are there circumstances in which you are in danger of being a 'defective presence'?
- In what ways do you seek to honour those you work alongside?
- Are there any insights in this chapter that you want to take forward in your praxis?

8

Shame in Teaching and Learning

Introduction

The event that triggered my desire to study shame happened in formal education. I do not have a similar experience from my childhood experience in Sunday School or other Christian groups; they were usually safe places for me as I enjoyed learning. However, I know that is not the experience of everyone, and has not always been my experience when studying as an adult. Ministerial training, which was the impetus for this study of shame, was a very different experience to anything else I have ever done. Reports that go to your bishop (in an Anglican context) are very personal and much more about who you are than what you can do. It is not difficult to feel misunderstood and misrepresented and to experience shame for seemingly not being able to communicate some of the essence of your calling. I am saying this as someone who had no issues highlighted to work on in my training or first role after ordination, but still some shame was triggered in me. Shame in educational contexts is not unusual as often they are about becoming and that reflects our identity rather than our actions. Poling observes that 'too often ministries of teaching and care are based on perpetuating dominant values and maintaining boundaries that exclude marginal experiences and groups. Teaching children to obey Jesus can reinforce their silence about secret suffering' (1991, p. 186). Ministers can sometimes exacerbate shame because there is *'a lack of self-awareness in clergy of what they are doing and its effects on people, or even because of clergy lacking a clear enough self-identity to deal with people expressing views or supporting practices contrary to their views'.*

Ministry is not easy and shame can be experienced by both the teacher and learner.

Shame can happen at every level in teaching and learning. It is not uncommon in people studying for a doctorate to experience what is known as imposter syndrome, feeling they will be found out to be a fraud and they have no right to be where they are. This can be experienced in ministerial training too with a feeling that 'if they knew what I was really like they would never have accepted me'. Learners are often making themselves vulnerable, and can struggle in many different ways where shame may be a consequence. It is important to realize that whenever we are doing some training or education, and to be mindful of the power of our role.

Conscientization – raising awareness of shame in ministry

One of the things I am now committed to is raising awareness of shame as part of my teaching in different contexts. My research suggests that ministers in training receive very different amounts of input on shame and this might be in modules on cross-cultural mission or pastoral care or even integrated across different modules. Freire (1996, p. 100) uses the term 'conscientization' for this and it is part of the role of the educator. I educate people for ministry as well as being part of a church leadership team. My own experience as well as my research has highlighted some of the ways that being in ministry can trigger shame. The first is around self-perception and includes such things as:

- never feeling good enough;
- dissonance between how we present on the outside and the reality of life;
- difference between intellectual and emotional responses to issues, such as '*I know I don't have to be perfect but feel like I do*';
- frustration at giving into temptation and feeling like we should have done better;
- difficult passions that cannot be controlled.

The second area of difficulty relates to religious dimensions of our ministry:

- feeling of causing displeasure to God;
- thinking our prayer life is inadequate;
- not measuring up to standards of holiness.

A third area involves others:

- congregational pressure to be perfect;
- difference in standards between what we expect of others and of ourselves;
- expectations of the family;
- false ideas about discipleship;
- loss of faith;
- not understanding what it means to be a public representative of Christ.

Thus, when we are teaching we may be bringing some of this baggage with us and it may impact how we teach, the content of it and what we communicate through how we come across. It is important that educators 'come to know their own shame, not because it was a requirement of their training, but because it was utterly necessary to their lives, and their own emotional healing' (Lloyd and Sieff 2015, p. 36). There are many topics where shame could be included as part of the training in areas such as diversity, communication, leadership, discipling, interpersonal communication and management, for example. It is the sort of subject better integrated into a range of modules perhaps than the focus of one as processing our shame is often an ongoing task and shame can be triggered in a range of contexts.

Formation and facilitating the development of a non-shaming culture

Formation is an integral part of training for ministry. For those of us doing the training, we need to be mindful of helping students find healthy ways of dealing their own shame so they can deal with others but also to try to create a non-shaming culture. Being judgemental is something all of us can slip into and remembering that our first response is often the one that is remembered and this should be compassionate. While training for ministry there may well be issues that need exploring or addressing and certainly it is important for anything that may impede the journey towards ordination to be discussed, but this should be done appropriately. One person comments: '*If it is necessary to challenge someone, it should be done in a transparent way, with privacy and a chance for them to respond and discuss the best way forward.*' Another suggests: '*Try very hard not to judge; an outward persona may hide a very different person.*' We are sometimes quick to judge without understanding and may try to put shame on to other people because they do not fit our expectations of what a 'good' ordinand, lay minister, youth worker etc. may be. This still happens over cultural issues such as appearance or dress.

In researching this topic it became clear that there are still issues for some in men and women working alongside each other in relation to what is known as the 'Billy Graham rule' (see Sharman 2018). Some of the outworking of this role can end up being shaming for either the man or woman concerned and perhaps logically should be extended to never be alone with anyone. Some, including me, have experienced scripture being used negatively against them and looking at hermeneutical perspectives that affirm women's ministry has been important for many women clergy.

The threads that came through most strongly from church members in their advice to ministers were about leaving judging to God; creating space for dialogue; and encouraging people to respond as Jesus did. This comment was emblematic of the responses:

> *Read and digest the Gospels and let Jesus' actions and words shape and challenge your own. Focus on compassion and mercy rather than trying to make people conform or behave*

as you think they should. However, also be bold in challenging people when they themselves are acting in ways which shame or embarrass others, e.g. being judgemental, declaring who God finds unacceptable. Be slow to criticize others and be willing to confess your own faults publicly on occasion.

Helping those training for ministry work out what sort of minister they want to be is an integral part of formation and the theological educator's role. As one respondent suggested, '*Don't forget what it was like to be a member of the church without being in leadership.*' There is a difference between supporting one another to lead godly lives and judging and shaming others. However, as ministers we need to avoid feeling shame when we don't see the hoped-for change in individuals, groups or a congregation; God does not always work in the way we expect or with the timing we would like, we can only be responsible for what we ourselves do.

Modelling

For those of us whose ministry involves education and training, modelling a non-shaming culture is important. This is an important observation:

If people are being educated within a shaming culture then that is what the student will learn. For example, missing morning prayer is seen as shameful and this can be taken on by the fellow students, thinking they have a right to be questioning the issue without first understanding the reason why the student missed prayer. My experience at college was that it was easier to ask for forgiveness than permission, as permission was rarely granted. This in itself presents an unhealthy attitude.

In formational contexts attitudes and approaches may be caught as much as taught. It is challenging to work out how a formational process treats people as autonomous adults while ensuring accountability to a range of stakeholders who have expectations about the process. Examining my own praxis has helped me to work out the difference between encouraging appropriate professional behaviour, socializing people into what is expected and engendering a climate of fear around, for example, being late. I am also aware that my values and personality both lead to seeing timekeeping as an issue and I need to be aware of where my preferences may not be right in a particular context. Imposing values is a way of shaming others and one which is usually best avoided:

> *there is a need for clergy to be open-minded about what their theological values are and that they may differ to others. Even if they continue to disagree, this should be an opportunity for dialogue and learning rather than finger-pointing. There should be an understanding of the impact of labels that people carry (that aren't easily shaken off) when the finger has been pointed.*

I try to be equitable in my practice which means that sometimes I think I am seen as soft, but some students start so far back that they need some latitude and support to get to the place where they begin to fulfil their potential.

Challenging shaming behaviour when observed is important as this can model how to do it well. If it is not challenged, then it may appear that it is being condoned. I appreciate in writing this that there are a range of issues where there are strong opposing opinions but treating each other with respect and dignity should be foundational to all encounters.

I have been employed in ministry since 1984 but have found that since being ordained there are some distinctive issues that I did not experience previously. The ontological nature of being a priest means that I sometimes feel that my conduct is unpriestly and I feel more shame at some thoughts and actions than I have done in the past. While I have always sought to be consistent in private and public I am more aware of the implications of my behaviour when I have a dog collar on, as in essence I am a representative of God and the church and I am aware that generalizations may be made out of what has been observed of me. This is perhaps the significant difference for clergy – they are more exposed, more vulnerable and perhaps more judged than other professionals, particularly if they live among the communities they serve. It is perhaps helpful to be reminded of the way that God clothed Adam and Eve when they became aware of their nakedness. Thus, while as clergy we may feel more acutely a fear of exposure, of a metaphorical nakedness and sense of helplessness, that God has compassion on us and will meet us at our point of need is important to remember and communicate.

Positive practices as an educator

Within training for many caring profession roles there is the potential for shaming. Bond (2009) talks about connecting and disconnecting behaviour as a helpful lens through which to explore our praxis. One of the temptations we may face is to correct learners in front of others in such a way as to encourage the group to comply with the agreed norms of behaviour. Discipline in learning contexts can be a difficult topic: unless some boundaries are adhered to, it can be difficult for people to learn. In my educational context we would usually try to negotiate and agree ground rules with students and sometimes then groups will self- or peer-regulate in relation to them. However, it is usually less shaming to talk to someone out of the earshot of others if they are behaving in a way which is not helpful. I encourage students to share openly or privately if there is a situation which is distracting them and which may necessitate them having to take a telephone call (e.g. a sick child or car recovery service).

In adult education contexts emphasising competition between students is usually not appropriate, particularly over grades or 'successful' performance. I am often aware in my theological setting that someone who got a grade 30 marks below the top student may have achieved more than the person with 80 per cent because of where they started from. Ministry is collaborative in nature and encouraging working together, particularly with those who are very different from each other, can be much more valuable. Relational competence is often more useful in ministry than academic competence.

One of the things I commend people for is asking for help. I try to communicate that there is no question too basic to ask about a topic we are studying and that if one person has a question there are often several others sitting there thinking the same thing. Sometimes it is tempting to tell people off for not asking for help but what may be necessary is identifying some of the reasons for not doing so and trying to mitigate against them. Shame at not knowing or listening, for example, may be an issue for some and flight or fright are regular responses in educational contexts. Helping people to identify their own default positions can help them understand some of the potential barriers to learning. One of the comments that concerns me is when people say they didn't want to disturb me because I am so busy. I am always happy to respond to a question or request for help in an area which is a primary responsibility.

In any educational or learning setting there are going to be power dynamics at play, particularly if there is any form of assessment involved. Shaming sometimes occurs with too authoritarian a style which leaves learners feeling intimidated or fearful, and this can result in them being unable or unwilling to speak or respond. It may also cause dissonance if the educator is too dogmatic over what the learner needs to believe. There are very few topics where there is no possible alternative interpretation and the fact that someone is disagreeing with us is not a reason to shame them.

Many of the issues I encounter as barriers to learning are in the affective domain, the emotional responses. But this means that we need to give time to support learners to overcome anxiety or other issues. There is a lot of talk about wanting to widen the diversity of those in ministry or leadership roles but for some there may be a lot of baggage to overcome because of previous poor responses or lack of encouragement. We may need to be prepared to walk alongside individuals as they seek to enhance their learning and education in a more formal way. Even those who feel well equipped in a previous vocation or other contexts can feel disempowered in ministerial training where it sometimes feels as if what they bring with them is not valued.

Developing resilience in leadership in theological education in relation to shame

Roles as an educator can be challenging for many reasons, including expectations, available resources, pressure to conform to stakeholders' desires and many other things. Developing resilience is a valuable attribute. Although the original research this list is based on was done with women in evangelical settings in the USA, I think it has broader application and am thus sharing it here. Resilience in leadership involved:

- disrupting systems that used shame to endorse gendered roles for leadership;
- naming fear and anger;
- empowering others and one's own agency;
- facing into experiences of shame;
- employing leadership styles appropriate to the institutional and leadership culture;
- making choices to step out of leadership and/or change contexts;
- being responsive to self and others in face of criticism;
- awareness of the influence of shame in learning;
- standing out and being seen.

(Tillman-Samuelson 2018, p. 223)

Levels of collegiality as opposed to competition can determine how this is experienced. I have found that when working in good teams there is a corporate resilience which helps you to overcome some of the challenges, as well as opportunities for humour which can ameliorate stress a little at times.

Bonhoeffer on asking questions

On my journey as an educator there have been lightbulb moments; reading Bonhoeffer (2006) on what it means to tell the truth was one of them (see Nash 2016). Although this is only a fragment of an essay written while Bonhoeffer was in prison, it has made me think about how I teach and engage in ministry. I don't want to be a person who asks the wrong or unjustified question and inadvertently causes someone to experience shame. Bonhoeffer asks if we are justified in demanding someone answer our question truthfully. This may seem a strange thing to say as on the surface it may always seem right to expect a truthful answer. However, we exist within a context and our encounters may often have an ethical element. Much education is done in groups and asking a question orally will usually lead to an oral answer which means everyone else gets to hear it. Bonhoeffer argues that 'the more diverse the life circumstances of people are, the more responsibility they have and the more difficult it is "to tell the truth"' (2006, p. 602). I became very aware of that as I wrote about my own experiences of shame. It was important to me to focus on my own reactions and circumstances, not tell stories about identifiable people to whom I had never talked about an incident and who had not been given an opportunity to explain their perspective on it. This means that we need to learn how to tell the truth in any given situation, which for Bonhoeffer involves expressing what is real but in an orientation that is Godward and involves the essence of truth not the appearance of truth. He sees indiscriminate truth-telling as destructive. Most people know that the answer to the question 'Does my bum look big in this?' is usually going to be 'No', regardless of whether or not that is a true statement, and a straight 'yes' is likely to be hurtful, notwithstanding cultural trends where the right answer might be 'Yes' and 'No' is the wrong one. Bonhoeffer's example was a school teacher asking a question of a pupil about whether their father often came home drunk which he believed was not appropriate for the teacher to ask. The pupil may have felt shame in answering it, potentially vicarious shame on behalf of their father but also for him or herself being labelled as the child of a drunk. The pupil denied it and Bonhoeffer argues that this was the right thing to do as it was a violation of the privacy of the family. Bonhoeffer suggests there are three elements to take into consideration:

- recognizing who calls on me to speak and what authorizes me to speak;
- recognizing the place in which I stand;
- putting the subject I am speaking about into this context.

(Bonhoeffer 2006, p. 608)

In essence, we need to be mindful about what is appropriate to say in a particular time, place, context and role.

There are times, perhaps more in pastoral than educational contexts, where we might be tempted to ask questions out of our own curiosity rather than because they are illuminating. Bonhoeffer calls someone who indiscriminately tells the truth without regard for the individual they are talking to a cynic and argues this destroys truth between people. He argues that such a person 'violates shame, desecrates the mystery, breaks trust, betrays the community in which he lives, and smiles arrogantly over the havoc he has wrought and over the human weakness that "can't bear the truth"' (2006, p. 602). When I teach on something controversial or personal I always try to make it clear that people need to answer at the level at which they feel safe within the group. I do not pick on people to answer questions and, if I want everyone to contribute, I give warning of this so there is time to formulate an answer people feel comfortable sharing. I am also mindful of the potential with some topics of answers triggering others in the group who are not comfortable with a topic or who were not expecting it to be raised.

Reflection questions

- Have you ever experienced shame in a learning context? What triggered it? How did you process it? Did you address it with the person who shamed you?
- Looking at the areas of shame for ministers, which ones have you seen or experienced? What was the impact of them?
- What is your reaction to Bonhoeffer's perspective on truth telling?
- Can you think of a leader who models a non-shaming culture? What have you learnt from them?
- Are there any changes you want to make in your praxis as a consequence of reading this chapter?

9

Creating a Less Shaming Church

Case study:

Creating a less shaming church by Daniel Corcoran

It's beginning to look a lot like that most wonderful time of the year when people expect to hear about Jesus. School children minister the nativity story to parents and carols are playlisted everywhere among secular favourites. And we make the most of every opportunity ensuring our words are stuffed fuller with grace than the turkey is with chestnuts and seasoned with more salt than the roasties, knowing that among all the lights and glory, feelings of darkness and shame often intensify. Ears are surprisingly open to hear of God's lavish love, persistent presence, active attentiveness, gushing grace, fresh forgiveness, profound purposes, masterminded meaning and crucial connection with the shamed and broken. In terms of Christmas Gospel connection, I wish it could be Christmas every day . . . until my 'how is this understood' radar pings in worship signalling danger zones which wouldn't appear in conversation or preaching. I blame a background in information literacy for this radar, equipped with Myers-Briggs ISFP-type sensitivity prompting conversations that warn how church expression, both verbal and physical, can inadvertently (or even purposefully) re-stitch Good Friday's torn curtain compromising the freedom and confidence encouraged in relating to God.

Emma is a Communications Officer working with many vulnerable people where I was Mission Priest. She is confused.

At a Christmas event she loved hearing that God is with her but at a Christmas service the first words were, 'May the Lord be with you'. She wondered if God had to be summoned by a minister. After a song welcoming Jesus into the place, the minister prayed '. . . so God, please be with us now' and she wondered why the church didn't believe he already was. Emma asked why the church packaged this good news in wishy-washy language normally found in cheap greetings cards. We talked about the uncertain flavour of the word 'may', the historic and regional understandings of how 'be' usually means 'is', and where the phrase comes from in Scripture . . . and so on.

We were developing a community literacy policy with the the National Literacy Trust (https://literacytrust.org.uk/) to make local community services (including our own) more accessible and Emma's church experiences led to further conversations about misunderstandings in worship. Emma also felt that dependency on the minister 'to make it all happen' was immensely disempowering especially for those trapped in damaging relationships. She therefore suggested the less ambiguous and more empowering 'The Lord is with you' or 'Thank you for being with us' would help enormously when beginning services.

If only we were as confident about the gospel in worship as we are in mission. The fact that the two feel different highlights the presence of this repaired curtain. On one side of the tracking we confidently proclaim who God is and what he does; on the other, we seem to suspend this confidence and pray for God to be who he is and do what he is doing. On both sides a surprising distrust in Emmanuel's nature exists, fuelling prayers for our 'with-us God' to be with us. While God invites us to pray as we feel and hears everything from eloquent tones, frustrated moans to inexplicable groans, in public worship we could enable greater faith and confidence in God by thanking God for his already given-gifts – as Paul encourages us to do – rather than asking for them as if they have never been given. It is rather odd to ask for what one has already been given and more usual to be grateful.

Steve was the School Counsellor where I once worked. He wasn't a Christian but at a pupil's baptism at a Baptist church he was interested in the Confession as he was researching the healing nature of forgiveness at the time. He liked this opportunity to deal with failure and hear promises of forgiveness read from the Bible. He said his case-load would lessen if everyone forgave and if only everyone could hear words of assured forgiveness this would help relieve people's root feelings of guilt and shame.

If only indeed. Helen felt she was drowning in a whirlpool of shame and finds hearing about God's forgiveness and prayers of confession helpful and hopeful. She felt that the Absolution was an anti-climax leaving her still drowning. We talked through the words and discovered that in fourteen of the fifteen absolutions in Common Worship the Minister is simply asking for forgiveness all over again and only one states, 'receive God's pardon and peace'. Despite David (Psalm 103.8–12) and Micah (7.18–20) even proclaiming God's forgiveness in the Old Testament, despite overwhelming New Testament promise of forgiveness and despite the Reformation turning Absolution from precatory wishes into proclamation, today we have settled with precatory wish and reticence to pronounce God's forgiveness with clarity.

To a society more used to unforgiveness and grudges, 'God forgives you' is tangibly life-giving and refreshing. We presume we communicate this in liturgy, but we do not. Some may have sufficient biblical and liturgical literacy and knowledge of God's generous nature to presume that the Absolution means we are forgiven. However, those who are not are left uncertain and pushed further away from receiving promised forgiveness. Due to liturgical phraseology, a very thick curtain exists for the many who presume 'he wouldn't forgive someone like me after what I've done'. Therefore, we demand far more faith, literary understanding and presumptuousness from those who may not possess these things and who are drowning in shame to be able to extract the words 'God forgives you' from the words 'May God forgive you' than from those who know of God's loving nature and can autocorrect 'May God forgive you' and presume it means 'God forgives you'. If the Absolution simply told Helen and others 'God forgives you', we would not have a re-stitched curtain full of inexplicable grammar and syntax.

Bishop Paul Butler, when Bishop of Southwell and Nottingham, said the simplest and most effective absolution Helen has ever heard which assured of God's forgiveness, prompted the forgiving of others and herself. It 'provided a rope from God to help pull me from shame'. It is simply 'God forgives you, so forgive others and forgive yourself'. Helen and others of all ages expressed in conversation afterwards how they have never heard God's forgiveness stated so clearly.

Back to Christmas

A faithful Intercessor led prayers for the world and community and Emma wondered why we ask God to hear them and assumes that if we can't presume that God is with us, we can't presume on his hearing either. If only we thanked God for hearing instead. Even though David states his assurance of God's attentiveness (Psalm 6.9 and Psalm 66.19), liturgy suggests a possibility that God may neither hear nor accept prayers, especially if dependent on reminding God of his mercy following an ambiguous absolution. Praying to God to hear and accept prayers made possible through his gift of prayer holds prayer out of reach from those who would never presume that God would hear them – those whose lives could be transformed – like Emma's – through knowing of God's absolute attentiveness. Sadly, experiences like these meet clerical responses such as 'how could anyone think that?', 'don't try to explain liturgy – just let it do its work', 'we mustn't be presumptuous towards God' and even 'is she stupid?' as if we can do no wrong in church. Emma is far from stupid and I believe issues a warning to how we conduct ourselves in worship. There is, of course, irony in someone explaining that liturgy should not be explained, and those discouraging presumptuousness towards God presume that their prayers are heard. There is also sadness about the lack of pastoral or missional concern for those who we fail through prioritizing one's love of misleading liturgy over God's love of people.

It's time for the final song, 'Away in a manger'. And it's lovely. Isn't it?

I am asked one day in school, 'will God only love me if I ask him right?' I reply, quite overwhelmed, that no one needs to ask because God has loved him even before he was born and he will never stop loving him, ever. The question came from a child who didn't feel loved at home and, believing this to be all his fault, he wanted to be sure that God loved him so that he could feel loved. His doubt came from verse 3 where we dare to teach children in their most formative years to ask the Lord Jesus to, 'be near me . . ., stay close by me forever and love me'. We would never explain to our child that they had to ask for our love, nor would we preach, 'You must ask God to love you before he will'. But this popular carol has taught generations around world that God's love and presence are dependent on our asking. How about we change the culture with a few word and punctuation changes?

You're with me Lord Jesus;
You've promised to stay close by me forever and love me.
I pray bless all the little children in your tender care . . .

The minister concludes the service with the words of 2 Corinthians 13.13 (the Grace). As the words 'may' and 'be' do not feature in the Greek we turn Paul's original encouraging statement of fact (see Robert Young's 1898 Literal Translation) into yet another prayer asking again for God's grace, love and presence. By this time no one is sure of receiving anything and we turn 'We love because he first loved us' (1 John 4.19) into 'He may love us if we ask him enough', as if we make the gospel happen ourselves.

All I want for Christmas is that we sing from the same carol sheet every day so that Emma, Steve and Helen and others in society who feel the same can know the curtain-free nature of God's love, presence, attentiveness and forgiveness, able to live with feet set on rock rather than drowning in a whirlpool of shame.

Church

Creating a less shaming church in part depends on how we see church. I have long had a passion for the church as Christ's body in the world and a desire to mediate that body in a way that reflects the loving, caring God. This is not to suggest that I don't believe in the concepts of sin and judgement but more that I grieve over the way that God and Christianity have been misrepresented and know how unhelpful some of that was for me as I was growing up. I am particularly concerned with how class and culture shape our Christianity in ways that are unhelpful and often shaming. One person commented:

> *The church is very middle class. As an overweight person I spent the first 25 years being looked down on and fat-shamed by well-meaning Christians. It was liberating to become part of working-class church where people just accept you for who you are – shaming behaviour is much less prevalent because most people are also failures in the eyes of others. They know what it means to be labelled, talked about, blamed, humiliated – so they don't do it! Middle-class church can learn a lot about what it means*

to be truly loved and accepted for who you are. If you love someone you don't try to control them (shaming form of controlling behaviour).

In seeking to understand church theologically Pembroke (2004) identifies four principles relating to God's covenant with humanity which are helpful in framing some of the key elements of church:

- a recognition of personhood;
- being proactive in meeting the needs of others (covenant was initiative of grace);
- prioritize those most at risk (biblical concern for orphan, alien and widow);
- the importance of internalizing the dominant vision to feel at home (assuming the dominant vision is healthy and life-affirming).

I would also want to be explicit about acting in a loving way towards self and others. Joining the institutional church changed my life for the better, giving me a vocation, community and place of belonging. I am sad when it does not do that for others. As Dykstra argues, 'in and through the church, God in Christ by the power of the Spirit actually makes people's lives better and stronger, more hospitable and gracious, more joyful, generous, and just' (2008, p. 42). Faith is a journey and my hope is for a church that welcomes people where they are on their journey and seeks to accompany them as they continue on the path.

Being a less shaming church will in part depend on how healthily the church functions. Capps (2002) suggests that these are principles to consider adopting:

- affirming and identifying our distinctiveness as individuals;
- knowing that disapproval can be expressed and how to do it;
- using open communication in a disciplined way;
- engendering a sense of solidarity and shared meaning;

- being open and welcoming to outsiders, forming a caring community;
- reflecting on experience and implementing any implications of this.

I would add that a clear structure that enables you to know who to talk to about what should include the capacity to provide feedback on leadership.

The church taking responsibility for ways it has shamed in the past can be significant in being less shaming in the future. It feels like there is a growing mistrust of institutions and a transparency over what happens is important. When something does go wrong which results in shaming of an individual or a group then corporate soul-searching to review what might have been missed or identify safeguards which could be put in place to avoid it happening again is important. Nelson (2016) argues that there are five practices that help to promote a shame-resistant or shame-transforming church:

- church leaders openly talk about shame;
- there is not a hierarchy of sin and shame;
- corporate sin is examined and confessed;
- public failure of Christians is responded to with grace and humility;
- the church welcomes those whose stories include their shame.

Styles of church leadership can have an impact on experiences of shame. One survey respondent commented: '*For me it's understanding how much I am forgiven that allows me to stop judging. Judging is also about not believing in a boundless forgiving God. If blame or finger-pointing does not come from the pulpit, or if a huge acceptance is modelled, I genuinely believe that the congregants follow suit.*' Anthropologist Martha Nussbaum argues that 'we need to protect spaces within which people explore and confront aspects of their humanity that are problematic and may occasion shame, whether to themselves or others' (2004, p. 296). This can need skilled facilitation, and a team approach to leadership with a variety of different roles and gifts makes this more likely. As one person suggested: '*I think there is an increasing need for people in leadership to recognize their need to surround themselves with a team who can contribute gifts they themselves do not have. This requires humility and a recognition of servant leadership.*' Perhaps what is most important is to be welcoming and hospitable, allowing those who have such gifts to create a culture where people do not feel a pressure to conform to a set of cultural norms which may be alienating or constraining and which are not relevant to being a follower of Jesus. However, there also needs to be an awareness that sometimes shame just happens as a consequence of being human, and having a healthy attitude towards it may be useful. Thus, Simon shared: '*At some point, way back when, I just made one of those decisions in life, I thought I'd far rather share my shame. I'm not hot on the whole confession route, I'd rather share my shame communally and with other people who are willing to share their shame.*' He strongly asserted that it is often an issue of we won't share our shame rather than can't. Openly talking about shame takes away its power but it is important to ensure that it is safe to do so. Sharing doubts and struggles may come into this category and while I don't see them as a source of shame, individuals sometimes have.

The God we mediate

What sort of God our church mediates can impact how people experience shame. One of the ways we may need to think about this in particular is any visual representations of Jesus as part of the fabric. What do the windows, pictures, icons etc. say to us about how we understand God, and most often the person of Jesus? I grew up in a church named after St Peter which was broadly helpful as it helped me understand that God forgives mistakes, even big ones like Peter made when he denied Jesus (Luke 22.54–62; John 21.15–25). The ethnicity of Jesus in some representations of him has historically been problematic – those born in the Middle East are not usually blonde with blue eyes! If God through word or image is most often seen as accusing, judgemental, remote, uncaring, uninterested, then this can be absorbed as feelings of shame and sinfulness. A lack of pictures of or including women can be problematic too. Asking what best communicates a merciful, gracious, loving, compassionate God is a question that may challenge our current church images and language. Gittins' description of Jesus helps us to see the full scope of the God we want to mediate if we want to be a less shaming church:

> God became a human being, incarnated in Jesus whose pastoral response was to take the initiative, to reach out, to touch, to cross boundaries, to include, to forgive, and to extend healing and hope. He refused to be cowed by rules which threatened him with contamination and pollution, or to apologize for his physical limitations and needs. He spoke intimately of God and proclaimed that God loves the imperfect in body, and that God's healing is intended to restore and to raise up those who are destroyed or abased. He refused to be paralyzed by fear. Women and children were religiously marginal, Jesus not only sought them out and embraced them, but called his followers to be as socially powerless as they were. People whose life were contaminated by bodily impurity, physical defect, or occupational messiness (menstruating women, lepers, prostitutes, or tax collectors) were not only befriended but explicitly assured they would be the first in God's kingdom (Matthew 20.31–32). Those who were simply invisible (the hungry, the thirsty, the naked, the sick, the imprisoned, the strangers) were dignified by being identified with Christ himself (Matthew 25.35ff). Furthermore, Jesus asserted that nothing that touches a person can pollute or contaminate, for sinful pollution comes only from within (Mark 7.14). Human persons can pollute, but bodies cannot be polluted. (Gittins 1999, p. 39)

This is a helpful overview which may benefit from being communicated in such a succinct way. Sometimes we do not fully appreciate the cumulative impact of the individual actions of Jesus to challenge that which may shame. The concept of the *imago Dei* which I discussed previously is also relevant. While often we may think of it in an individual way, we need to also consider it corporately too. Thus, 'people cannot find the image of God within themselves or others on their own. The image can only be constructed and seen with others through corporate effort and communion' (Pattison 2013, p. 156). How can we mediate a God whose image is found in everyone, making everyone precious, worthy of respect and honour?

The quality of relationships in a church is perhaps what will best help it to be a non-shaming environment or a place where shame is healed. Community, acceptance and belonging is important. Thus, 'finding relationships with significant others in which we experience some semblance of nurture and care without having to turn ourselves inside out, in ways that only increase our shame, in order to meet other people's expectations' (Wimberly 1999, p. 1). This can help keep people in church who might otherwise have walked away because of their shame. Small groups can sometimes provide this space as they give the opportunity to share our stories, be heard, accepted and loved. However, small groups can be the source of shame too in terms of whether or not people feel they can invite others into their home or feel uncomfortable and unsure how to behave in the homes of others. Perhaps considering a neutral venue may work best in some contexts. Social media can also provide an opportunity to remind people of their worth and value and that they are remembered and loved. High quality relationships are not a quick fix, and shame can take many years to overcome but such relationships are often a pre-requisite for someone to feel safe and begin to name and process their experiences. Pattison writes evocatively of what may be heard, and commends the capacity to embrace 'the brokenheartedness of frail humans rather than sin, guilt, and offense against a divine despot' (2011, p. 26). Culture setting is an important part of church and that includes our default understanding of who we are. Sometimes perspectives need to be changed and we need to adopt an identity based on who we are in God. This is not always the case; sadly 'Many people raised in Christian circles encounter rules, often implied, about how they should behave. Though it is ironic considering the term, legalism typically uses shame more than guilt to induce certain behaviors, people follow the rules to be accepted by the group' (Georges and Baker 2016, p. 118).

As part of a discussion of relationships, it is important to note some of the less helpful ways in which some people react, which exacerbates shame. There are a range of defensive responses that we need to be aware of and avoid ourselves. Rage and shame are often intimately linked; rage is a common response to shame and one which we may experience in a pastoral relationship. We also need to be aware of how rage may be triggered in us because of our own shame. Perfectionism is another response to shame and this can lead to disowning parts of ourselves which bring us shame and the development of a shadow (McNish 2004). Sometimes righteousness is an unhelpful response to shame in the church which can lead to trying to avoid or deny the shame. The elder son in the parable of the prodigal son (Luke 15.11–32) may illustrate this.

Shame examen

One of the tasks we may want to undertake is to reflect on the extent to which our church and ministerial praxis may be shaming. Ignatian spirituality has helped me to be more reflective in my faith. The examen is found in the writings of Ignatius of Loyola, a soldier who experienced a dramatic conversion to Christianity and who is best known for his spiritual exercises (Ignatius 1991). I have taken some of the core questions that are usually asked in the examen and adapted them to reflect on shame. I see this as an occasional thing to do for church ministers to think about in what ways their ministry may inadvertently shaming as well as more positive aspects.

Examen for ministers

Asking the Holy Spirit to guide us, reflecting back on the last period of time:

1 What ministerial praxis (actions, encounters, thoughts, feelings) do I feel most happy about? I will thank God for these experiences.
2 What ministerial praxis do I now feel discomfort about? I will ask for God's help to practise differently in the future, and, where appropriate, I will say that I am sorry.

Prompts to reflect on shaming praxis:

- Have my actions caused shame to those I minister alongside?
- In my interactions with individuals have I put pressure on them to comply or conform against their better judgement?
- Have I said or done anything to make someone feel that they are insufficient or not important?
- Do I act in ways that stigmatize or disempower?
- Are there ways in which the structures I am part of or represent are colluding with others which causes shame?
- Have the actions of my denomination or equivalent caused fragmentation leading to shame?
- Do I act in ways that are dissonant with my theology or that cause others to dissociate from the church?

Examen for church members

There may be times when it seems appropriate to ask a church member to reflect on their experiences of shame in the church. This could be done with a small group to reflect on corporate practices to see if there are changes needed. These are suggested questions:

Asking the Holy Spirit to guide us, reflecting back on experiences of church (in the past period of time):

1. What engagement with church do I feel most happy about? I will thank God for these experiences.
2. What engagement with church do I feel discomfort about? I will ask for God's help to deal with these feelings and remember that I am a unique human being created in the image of and loved by God and worthy of being treated with respect and dignity.

Prompts to reflect on shaming experiences:

- In my experience of church have I ever felt the need to conform or comply in ways which have caused me shame?
- Have I ever been made to feel that I am insufficient or not important?
- Are there times I feel shame because of the ways in which church leaders have acted?
- Have I ever felt stigmatized or disempowered in my encounters with church?
- Are there ways in which the structures of the church collude or fragment which causes me shame?
- Do any theological issues cause me dissonance or to dissociate from the church?

With the questions for both members and ministers it can be helpful to share the outcomes with someone who has pastoral skills or within a well facilitated group, as sometimes realizing what others experience helps us with ours.

Developing shame resilience

Shame resilience is a term often associated with Brené Brown who suggests that it is 'that ability to recognize shame when we experience it, and move through it in a constructive way that allows us to maintain our authenticity and grow from our experiences' (2008, p. 31).

It may be a useful concept as we consider how to be a less shaming church. In developing this theory Brown suggests that shame is a 'psycho-social-cultural construct' (2006, p. 45) which she sees as being part of a continuum with shame, fear, blame and disconnection on one side and empathy, courage, compassion and connection on the other (Brown 2008). Brown suggests a series of steps which can be helpful:

- recognizing shame, the flawed identities which come with it and the responses to it such as moving towards and appeasing, withdrawing or a more aggressive moving against;
- practising critical awareness – contextualizing, normalizing and demystifiying shame experiences;
- reaching out through sharing our story;
- speaking shame including our feelings and needs.

Missing within Brown's writing is a more theological element which is addressed by Poling's understanding of resilience. This involves our 'search for the resilient hope of the human spirit, which can resist abuse and create new communities for the restoration of communion and freedom of self, others, and God' (1991, p. 33). This is a more communal understanding reinforcing the importance of the kind of church we create.

Conclusion

Creating a less shaming church is a process rather than a series of one-off activities or decisions. It is also contextual as the shame felt will partly depend on who is in our congregation. I have spent quite a bit of time in recent years seeking to reassure the quite elderly that they are valuable, that they are appreciated, that we enjoy them being part of us – in the face of diocesan vision statements which they assume mean that the young are who is wanted in church. However, there are basic choices that we can make which are significant as this response identifies: '*Openness and authenticity. A lot of the shame I have experienced has come from secret places where people are worried about opening up or are not willing to talk about their true beliefs for fear of shame. Often people are worried about talking about their beliefs if they do not mirror those stereotypically held by church leaders.*' I conclude this chapter with a challenge from John Swinton which encompasses what I hope this book makes a small contribution to:

> The task of a liberating church is to reveal signs and pointers to remind the world that the way it is, is not the way it should be, and that loving 'the outsider' is not an act of charity, or a function of 'specialist ministries,' but is, in fact, a 'new' way of being human. In remembering God's actions in history, and in the life, death and resurrection of Christ, the Christian community is drawn into a new way of living and seeing the world. (Swinton 2000, pp. 125–6)

Reflection questions

- Which parts of the case study did you resonate with?
- Are there other ways in which Christmas can cause shame?
- What are your top three priorities in creating a less shaming church?
- Complete the shame examen. What emerges for you?
- Who in your context would be supportive about identifying ways in which you may be inadvertently shaming people and addressing this?
- What strengths do you have in relation to being able to support those who are shamed?
- How might you develop shame resilience?
- What changes in your praxis does this chapter encourage you to consider?

Appendix 1

Defining Shame in Relation to the Literature

This appendix shows where in the literature I identified different elements of shame for those who would like to read more widely.

An eclectic/synthesizing approach to defining shame (Pattison 2000, p. 52) includes some of these elements:

- shame can be both healthy and unhealthy (Bradshaw 2005);
- shame can be seen as the opposite of pride (Scheff 1979);
- shame can be felt anywhere over anything and it changes over time and culture (McNish 2003; Pembroke 2002);
- shame is culturally and chronologically interpreted (Lynd 1958);
- shame is what particularly distinguishes humanity from other creatures (Schneider 1992);
- shame involves an audience even if that is an idealized self (Pembroke 2002);
- there is a difference between feeling shame and shaming used as a social sanction (Bechtel 1991);
- shame as a family of meanings and phenomena cannot be reduced to a single definition and may be hard to identify and distinguish from guilt (Pattison 2000);
- shame has physiological, cognitive and behavioural consequences and affects our ability to think clearly, talk and act (Lewis 1995);

- shame is distinguishable from guilt which is about discrete actions, whereas shame encompasses the whole self (Pembroke 2002);
- shame is often associated with blushing or with turning away or hiding our face. It is sometimes masked behind anger, contempt, depression, superiority or denial (Morrison 1996).

Defining shame in different disciplines

I have chosen representative definitions from a range of disciplines that are usually drawn on by practical theologians. Within psychology and related disciplines definitions of shame are mainly individualistic. Ferguson, a psychologist, suggests that 'shame can be broadly understood as individuals' intense disappointment concerning their own or another's shortcomings, which they perceive as discrepant from standards of significance to them or important others' (2005, p. 378). From the perspective of pastoral care and counselling, Wimberly offers this succinct definition: 'feeling unlovable, that one's life has a basic flaw in it' (1999, p. 11). In the field of psychotherapy: 'Shame is a deeply held, embodied and implicit belief that there is something wrong and defective with who we are. It sits as a black hole at the centre of our being' (Lloyd and Sieff 2015, p. 27). A definition which focuses more on the discretion element is that 'shame guards the separate, private self with its boundaries and prevents intrusion and merger. It guarantees the self's integrity. At the same time, it also protects the integrity of the human relationship and prevents compete isolation and rejection' (Wurmser 1997, p. 65).

Other disciplines that have something to contribute to understanding shame include anthropology, which sees it as 'a painful emotion responding to a sense of failure to attain some ideal state' (Nussbaum 2004, p. 184). Sociologist Scheff sees shame as the major emotion because 'of its ubiquity in human experience, its role as the force behind conscience, and as the regulator of all of our emotions, including shame itself' (2011, p. 34). Pembroke, a pastoral theologian, combines elements of these definitions: 'Shame arises when the self evaluates itself as flawed, defective, inferior' (2002, p. 142) and goes on to suggest that judging that a cherished ideal has not been reached, a gap is perceived between the self as it is and the identity desired. There are some commonalities within these definitions which reinforce that shame is about perceptions of self and has an element of being comparative. Shame can be seen as including the following components: social or external cognitive; internal self-evaluative; emotional; behavioural; physiological (Gilbert 2002, pp. 5–6).

There is a reasonable consensus in the literature from a variety of disciplines regarding distinguishing shame and guilt: guilt tends to focus on what we have done and is oriented towards others, shame is oriented towards and impacts our sense of self (Goodliff 2005; Lynd 1958). Thus, shame is addressed by changing our thinking about ourselves, possibly leading to personal transformation, but guilt is addressed by thinking that may lead to changed behaviour and/or reparation (Woien et al. 2003, p. 314). Erikson suggests that the psychosocial crisis involving shame (autonomy *versus* shame and doubt) precedes the initiative *versus* guilt crisis and both of them happen in early childhood (1995, p. 245). Interestingly, reflecting on an institutional context, Erikson goes on to note how there is a limit to the extent to which a child or an adult can endure endless demands to perceive themselves as 'evil and dirty' (p. 227) and to see those who impose such judgements as infallible, so they may begin to 'consider as evil only the fact that they exist' (p. 228). Recognizing the early origins of shame and guilt in human development, and the capacity of this development to be stalled or malfunction, may be important in exploring shame that is experienced at a later date.

Consequences of shame

Positive

- A reminder to behave in a particular way in context (Goodliff 2005).

- Helps maintain privacy and boundaries in relationships (McNish 2003).
- Moral motivation to act appropriately (Pembroke 2002).

Negative:

- *Negative feelings* such as paralyzed, helpless, passive (Lewis 1971); unlovable and worthless (Wimberley 1999); exposed (McNish 2004); flawed, defective and inferior (Pembroke 2002); weak, inadequate, a loser, dirty, infantile (Nathanson 1987); fear of abandonment (Nathanson 1987); woundedness (Malina 2001);
- *Negative self-perceptions* such as feeling small and shrinking (Tangney and Dearing 2002); painfully diminished (Kaufman 1985); defective and unworthy (Fowler 1996); sense of self-respect doubted (Jacoby 1996); cloud that follows us, feeling at heart of identity we are poison (McMillan 2006); inferiority complex (Scheff and Retzinger 2001); seeping sense of badness (Berecz 1998); threat to integrity (Rustomjee 2009); fundamentally deficient as a human (Kaufman 1985); contempt for self (Pembroke 2010); loss of face, fall from grace, being unfixable (McMillan 2006); threat to sense one can be at peace in the world (Capps 2002);
- *Physiological or physical reactions* such as a desire to hide, crawl away or die (Lewis 1971); feeling of being watched (Capps 2002); potentially experiencing tears, rage or blushing (Lewis 1971); undischarged hostility including feeling rage towards someone then turning it back on self (Lewis 1971); getting trapped in a shame–rage–revenge cycle (Scheff and Retzinger 2001).

Shame in institutions

Anthropologist Mary Douglas called one of her books *How Institutions Think* and suggests that an institution 'provides the categories of their thought, sets the terms for self-knowledge, and fixes identities' (1987, p. 112) and shame may be part of these. Some of the ways in which shame has been seen communally include:

- Shame may have a national character with shame–rage–revenge cycles which have a potential for war or conflict (Wurmser 1994; Scheff and Retzinger 2001);
- Particular groups are seen as polluting, which can act as a thread to the social bond and impact community cohesion (Pattison 2011; Scheff and Retzinger 2001);
- Organizational effectiveness is impacted through such things as collective shame (as a response to a group action) or psychological distancing from the institution as a consequence of vicarious shame (Chi et al. 2015; Clough 2010; Shepherd et al. 2013);
- Shame can cause a loss of status, place, identity (Binau 2006; Malina 2001).

Appendix 2

Overview of Themes from the Research in Relation to the Typology

Typology Context	*Personal*	*Relational/ Associational Vicarious*	*Communal*	*Structural*	*Theological*	*Historical*
Church	Commitment to and participation; Bad leadership practices; Christian practices; Discipline	Bad behaviour of leaders; Public statements by church; Negative or unloving attitudes	Theological tradition; Processes; Church practices; Bad leadership	Church practices; Doctrinal or ecclesiological differences; Bad behaviour; Power	Appearing unloving; Doctrinal differences; Failure	Bury
Self	Expectation failure; Moral and ethical; Behavioural		Issues re fit or belonging or inadequacy		Compromising views	Wait until time seems right to deal with it

Typology Context	*Personal*	*Relational/ Associational Vicarious*	*Communal*	*Structural*	*Theological*	*Historical*
Others	Diminution or exclusion; Difference; Theology; Unwitting Appropriate conviction	Cultural images	Dissonance; Attitudes; Cultural values	Cultural issues		
Response	Fight or flight; Feeling judged	Fear of taint by association	Act to promote unity; Revisit core principles	Leaving church; Switch denomination	Flight or fight	Mistrust; Conflict

References and Further Reading

Albers, R. H. (1995), *Shame: A Faith Perspective*, New York: The Haworth Pastoral Press.

Alison, J. (1998), *The Joy of Being Wrong*, New York: Herder & Herder.

Arnold, B. T. (2008), *Genesis*, Cambridge: Cambridge University Press.

Avrahami, Y. (2010), 'בוש in the Psalms – Shame or Disappointment', *Journal for the Study of the Old Testament*, 34(3), pp. 295–313.

Bailey, W. M. (2013), *The Self-Shaming God Who Reconciles*, Eugene, OR: Pickwick Publications.

Bartchy, S. S. (2002), 'The Historical Jesus and Honor Reversal at the Table', in W. Stegemann, B. J. Malina and G. Theissen, eds, *The Social Setting of Jesus and the Gospels*, Minneapolis: Fortress Press, pp. 175–83.

Bechtel, L. M. (1991), 'Shame as a Sanction of Social Control in Biblical Israel: Judicial, Political, and Social Shaming', *Journal for the Study of the Old Testament*, 16(49), pp. 47–76.

Bechtel, L. M. (1993), 'Rethinking the Interpretation of Genesis 2.4b–3.24', in A. Brenner, ed., *A Feminist Companion to Genesis*, Sheffield: Sheffield Academic Press, pp. 77–117.

Bechtel, L. M. (1994), 'The Perception of Shame within the Divine–Human Relationship in Biblical Israel', in L. M. Hopfe, ed., *Uncovering Ancient Stones*, Winona Lake: Eisenbrauns, pp. 79–82.

Beck, R. (2011), *Unclean*, Eugene, OR: Cascade Books.

Berecz, J. M. (1998), *Beyond Shame and Pain*, Lima, Ohio: CSS Publishing.

Berne, E. (1964), *Games People Play: The Psychology of Human Relationships*, New York: Ballantine Books.

Berry, J. (2009), *Ritual Making Women: Shaping Rites for Changing Lives*, London: Equinox.

Berryman, J. W. (2009), *Teaching Godly Play*, Denver: Morehouse Education Resources.

Binau, B. A. (2006), 'Administrative Ministry: A Link Between Shame and Stress', *Trinity Seminary Review*, 27(2), pp. 99–106.

Bond, M. E. (2009), 'Exposing Shame and its Effect on Clinical Nursing Education', *Journal of Nursing Education*, 48(3), pp. 132–40.
Bonhoeffer, D. (1955), *Ethics*, trans. N. H. Smith, London: SCM Press.
Bonhoeffer, D. (2006), 'What is Truth?', in *Dietrich Bonhoeffer Works Vol. 16: Conspiracy and Imprisonment: 1940–1945*, Minneapolis: Fortress Press, pp. 601–08.
Borges, J. (2013), '"Dignified': An Exegetical Soteriology of Divine Honour', *Scottish Journal of Theology*, 66(1), pp. 74–87.
Bowlby, J. (1973), *Attachment and Loss: Separation: Anxiety and Anger* (Vol. 2), Harmondsworth: Penguin.
Bradshaw, J. (2005), *Healing the Shame that Binds You*, Deerfield Beach: Health Communications.
Brennan, L. and Binney, W. (2010), 'Fear, Guilt, and Shame Appeals in Social Marketing', *Journal of Business Research*, 63(2), pp. 140–6.
Brock, S. (1999), 'The Robe of Glory: A Biblical Image in the Syriac Tradition', *The Way*, 39(3), pp. 247–59.
Brown, B. (2006), 'Shame Resilience Theory: A Grounded Theory Study on Women and Shame', *Families in Society: The Journal of Contemporary Social Services*, 87(1), pp. 43–52.
Brown, B. (2008), *I Thought It Was Just Me (But It Isn't)*, New York: Gotham Books.
Brown, B. (2012, March), 'Listening to Shame', retrieved from: www.ted.com/talks/brene_brown_listening_to_shame?language=en.
Brueggemann, W. (2001), *The Prophetic Imagination* (2nd edn), Minneapolis: Fortress Press.
Caine, C. (2016), *Unashamed*, Grand Rapids: Zondervan.
Campbell, A. V. (1985), *Moderated Love: A Theology of Professional Care*, London: SPCK.
Campbell, A. V. (2003), 'Practical Theology as Virtuous Theology', *The Expository Times*, 114(9), pp. 291–5.
Capps, D. (2002), *Life Cycle Theory and Pastoral Care*, Eugene, OR: Wipf and Stock.
Carlin, N. S. (2005), 'Shame, Ministry and Theological Education: Leaves from the Notebook of a Defiant Seminarian', *Pastoral Psychology*, 53(6), pp. 501–14.
Carmichael, C. M. (1992), 'The Paradise Myth', in P. Morris and D. Sawyer, eds, *A Walk in the Garden: Biblical, Iconographical and Literary Images of Eden*, Sheffield: Sheffield Academic Press, pp. 47–63.
Catford, C. (2010), *How Might an Engagement with Spirituality Help One Suffering from Shame and Depression?* Unpublished dissertation, London: Heythrop College.
Chao, Y.-H., Cheng, Y.-Y. and Chiou, W.-B. (2011), 'The Psychological Consequence of Experiencing Shame: Self-sufficiency and Mood-repair', *Motivation and Emotion*, 35(2), pp. 202–10.

Chi, S. S., Friedman, R. A. and Lo, H. (2015), 'Vicarious Shame and Psychological Distancing Following Organizational Misbehavior', *Motivation and Emotion*, doi:10.1007/s11031-015-9483-0, pp. 1–18.

Cloud, H. (1990), *Changes That Heal*, Grand Rapids: Zondervan.

Clough, M. (2010), 'Shame and Organisations', *The International Journal of Leadership in Public Services*, 6(1), pp. 25–33.

Collicutt, J. (2012), 'Bringing the Academic Discipline of Psychology to Bear on the Study of the Bible', *Journal of Theological Studies*, 63(1), pp. 1–48.

Collicutt McGrath, J. (2009), *Jesus and the Gospel Women*, London: SPCK.

Collins, N. (2019), *Out of Control: Couples, Conflict and the Capacity to Change*, London: SPCK.

Common Worship (2000), www.churchofengland.org/prayer-and-worship/worship-texts-and-resources/common-worship/ministry/common-worship-ordination-services. Accessed 17 October 2019.

Connolly, H. (2002), *Sin*, London: Continuum.

Crouch, A. (2015), 'The Return of Shame', *Christianity Today*, 59(2), pp. 32–41.

Davidoff, F. (2002), 'Editorial: Shame: The Elephant in the Room', *Quality and Safety in Health Care*, 11(1), pp. 2–3.

deSilva, D. A. (2000), *Honor, Patronage, Kinship and Purity*, Downers Grove, IL: IVP.

deSilva, D. A. (2011), 'Turning Shame into Honor: The Pastoral Strategy of 1 Peter', in R. Jewett, W. L. Alloway Jr. and J. G. Lacey, eds, *The Shame Factor*, Eugene, OR: Cascade Books, pp. 159–86.

de Smet, A. (2007), 'Forgiveness: Making Some Connections Between Theology and Psychology, Preaching and Pastoral Practice', *Expository Times*, 119(3), pp. 116–19.

Douglas, M. (1966), *Purity and Danger*, London: Routledge.

Douglas, M. (1987), *How Institutions Think*, London: Routledge and Kegan Paul.

Duff, J., and Collicutt McGrath, J. (2006), *Meeting Jesus: Human Responses to a Yearning God*, London: SPCK.

Dykstra, C. (2008), 'Pastoral and Ecclesial Imagination', in D. C. Bass and C. Dykstra, eds, *For Life Abundant*, Grand Rapids: Eerdmans, pp. 41–61.

Erikson, E. H. (1995), *Childhood and Society* (2nd edn), London: Vintage.

Ferguson, J. K., Willemsen, E. W. and Castaneto, M. V. (2010), 'Centering Prayer as a Healing Response to Everyday Stress: A Psychological and Spiritual Process', *Pastoral Psychology*, 59(3), pp. 305–29.

Ferguson, T. J. (2005), 'Mapping Shame and Its Functions in Relationships', *Child Maltreatment*, 10(4), pp. 377–86.

Fitzmyer, J. A. (2008), *First Corinthians. The Anchor Yale Bible*, New Haven, CT: Yale University Press.

Ford, D. (2011), *The Future of Christian Theology*, Chichester: Wiley Blackwell.

Fowler, J. (1996), *Faithful Change: The Personal and Public Challenges of Postmodern Life*, Nashville, TN: Abingdon Press.

Freire, P. (1996), *Pedagogy of the Oppressed*, London: Penguin.

Georges, J., and Baker, M. D. (2016), *Ministering in Honor–Shame Cultures*, Downers Grove, IL: IVP Academic.

Gilbert, P. (2002), 'Body Shame: A Biopsychosocial Conceptualisation and Overview, with Treatment Implications', in P. Gilbert and J. Miles, eds, *Body Shame Conceptualisation, Research and Treatment*, Hove: Routledge, pp. 3–54.

Gittins, A. J. (1999), *Reading the Clouds*, Ligouri: Ligouri Publications.

Goffman, E. (1990), *Stigma: Notes on a Spoiled Identity*, London: Penguin.

Goldberg, C. (1991), *Understanding Shame*, Northvale: Jason Aronson.

Goodliff, P. (2005), *With Unveiled Face: A Pastoral and Theological Exploration of Shame*, London: Darton, Longman and Todd.

Gordon, R. P. (2015), *Genesis 1–11 in its Ancient Context*, Cambridge: Grove Books.

Graham, M. (2009), *Wanting to Be Her: Body Image Secrets Victoria Won't Tell You*, Grand Rapids: IVP.

Hay, J. (1995), *Donkey Bridges for Developmental TA*, Watford: Sherwood Publishing.

Ignatius of Loyola (1991), *Spiritual Exercises and Selected Works*, G. E. Ganss, ed., New York: Paulist Press.

Irenaeus (2015), *The Writings of Irenaeus*, trans. A. Roberts and W. H. Rambaut, Edinburgh: Aeterna Press.

Isherwood, L. (2004), 'The Embodiment of Feminist Liberation Theology: The Spiralling of Incarnation', *Feminist Theology*, 12(2), pp. 140–56.

Jacoby, M. (1996), *Shame and the Origins of Self-esteem*, Hove: Routledge.

Jamieson, P. D. (2016), *The Face of Forgiveness*, Downers Grove: IVP Academic.

Johnson, E. L., and Moran, P., eds (2013), *The Female Face of Shame*, Bloomington: Indiana University Press.

Kaufman, G. (1985), *Shame: The Power of Caring* (rev. edn), Cambridge, MA: Schenckman Publishing.

Kendrick, G. (1974), *How Much Do You Think You Are Worth?*, Tunbridge Wells: Make Way Music.

Kilborne, B. (2002), *Disappearing Persons*, Albany, NY: State University of New York Press.

King, M. L. (1968), *I've Been to the Mountain Top*, www.american-rhetoric.com/speeches/mlkivebeentothemountaintop.htm. Accessed 4 January 2015.

Knudsen, C. (1995), 'Understanding Congregational Dynamics', in N. M. Hudson and M. Laaser, eds, *Restoring the Soul of a Church*, Collegeville: The Liturgical Press, pp. 75–101.

Koepf-Taylor, L. W. (2013), *Give Me Children or I Shall Die: Children and Communal Survival in Biblical Literature*, Minneapolis: Fortress Press.

Kroeger, C. C., and Evans, M. J. (2002), *The IVP Women's Bible Commentary*, Downers Grove, IL: IVP.

Layder, D. (2004), *Social and Personal Identity*, London: Sage.

Leeming, D., and Boyle, M. (2011), 'Managing Shame: An Interpersonal Perspective', *British Journal of Social Psychology, DOI: 10.1111/j.2044-8309.2011.02061.x*, pp. 1–21.

Lewis, H. B. (1971), *Shame and Guilt in Neurosis*, New York: International Universities Press.

Lewis, M. (1995), *Shame The Exposed Self*, New York: The Free Press.

Lickel, B., Schmader, T., Curtis, M., Scarnier, M. and Ames, D. R. (2005), 'Vicarious Shame and Guilt', *Group Processes & Intergroup Relations*, 8(2), pp. 145–57.

Lloyd, L. D. and Sieff, D. F. (2015), 'Return from Exile', in D. F. Sieff, ed., *Understanding and Healing Emotional Trauma*, Hove: Routledge, pp. 25–44.

Lynd, H. (1958), *On Shame and the Search for Identity*, London: Routledge.

Malina, B. J. (2001), *The New Testament World: Insights from Cultural Anthropology*, Louisville, KY: Westminster John Knox.

Malina, B. J. (2010), 'Collectivism in Mediterranean Culture', in D. Neufeld and R. E. DeMaris, eds, *Understanding the Social World of the New Testament*, London: Routledge, pp. 17–28.

Malina, B. (2011), 'Anachronism, Ethnocentrism, and Shame: The Envy of the Chief Priests', in R. Jewett, W. L. Alloway Jr. and J. G. Lacey, eds, *The Shame Factor: How Shame Shapes Society*, Eugene, OR: Cascade Books, pp. 143–58.

McKeown, J. (2008), *Genesis The Two Horizons Old Testament Commentary*, Grand Rapids: Eerdmans.

McMillan, D. W. (2006), *Emotion Rituals*, New York, Routledge, 2006.

McNish, J. (2003), 'Shame's Revelatory and Transformative Potential, and Its Use and Misuse by the Church's Pastoral Ministry', *Pastoral Psychology*, 6(2), pp. 3–22.

McNish, J. L. (2004), *Transforming Shame: A Pastoral Response*, London: Routledge.

Meyers, C. L. (1993), 'Gender Roles and Genesis 3.16', in A. Brenner, ed., *A Feminist Companion to Genesis*, Sheffield: Sheffield Academic Press, pp. 118–41.

Middleton, J. R. (2005), *The Liberating Image*, Grand Rapids: Brazos.

Miller, W. I. (1997), *The Anatomy of Disgust*, Cambridge MA: Harvard University Press.

Mitroff, I. I. and Pauchant, T. (1990), *We're So Big And Powerful Nothing Bad Can Happen To Us*, New York: Birch Lane Press.

Morgan, M. L. (2008), *Shame*, London: Routledge.

Morrison, A. P. (1996), *The Culture of Shame*, New York: Ballantine Books.

Moschella, M. C. (2008), *Ethnography as a Pastoral Practice*, Cleveland: Pilgrim Press.

Nash, S. (2016), 'Shame in Pastoral Practice: Reflections in the Light of Field Research, Bonhoeffer and Godly Play', *Practical Theology*, 9(4), pp. 287–300.

Nash, S. (2018), *The Vulnerable Youth Worker*, Cambridge: Grove Books.

Nathanson, D. L., ed. (1987), *The Many Faces of Shame*, New York: Guilford Press.

Nathanson, D. L. (1992), *Shame and Pride*, New York: W. W. Norton and Co.

Nelson, H. D. (2016), *Unashamed*, Wheaton: Crossway.

Newbrough, J. R. (1995), 'Toward Community: A Third Position', *American Journal of Community Psychology*, 23(1), pp. 9–37.

Neyrey, J. H. (1998), *Honor and Shame in the Gospel of Matthew*, Louisville, KY: Westminster John Knox.

Neyrey, J. H. (2008), 'Loss of Wealth, Loss of Family, Loss of Honor: The Cultural Context of the Original Makarisms in Q', in J. H. Neyrey and E. C. Stewart, eds, *The Social World of the New Testament: Insights and Models*, Peabody: Hendrickson, pp. 87–102.

Nussbaum, M. C. (2004), *Hiding from Humanity: Disgust, Shame, and the Law*, Princeton: Princeton University Press.

O'Donohue, J. (1998), *Eternal Echoes Exploring our Hunger to Belong*, London: Transworld Publishers.

Osiek, C. (2008), 'Women, Honor, and Context in Mediterranean Antiquity', *HTS Teologiese Studies/Theological Studies*, 64(1), pp. 323–37.

Palmer, P. J. (1993), *To Know as We Are Known*, San Francisco: HarperSanFrancisco.

Pattison, S. (2000), *Shame: Theory, Therapy, Theology*, Cambridge: Cambridge University Press.

Pattison, S. (2011), 'Shame and the Unwanted Self', in R. Jewett, W. L. Alloway Jr. and J. G. Lacey, eds, *The Shame Factor: How Shame Shapes Society*, Eugene, OR: Cascade Books, pp. 9–29.
Pattison, S. (2013), *Saving Face: Enfacement, Shame, Theology*, Farnham: Ashgate.
Pembroke, N. (2002), *The Art of Listening: Dialogue, Shame and Pastoral Care*, Edinburgh, Continuum.
Pembroke, N. (2004), *Working Relationships: Spirituality in Human Service and Organisational Life*, London: Jessica Kingsley.
Pembroke, N. (2010), *Pastoral Care in Worship*, London: T and T Clark.
Percy, M. (2012), *The Ecclesial Canopy*, Farnham: Ashgate.
Pietersen, L. (2011), *Reading the Bible after Christendom*, Milton Keynes: Paternoster.
Poling, J. N. (1991), *The Abuse of Power*, Nashville, TN: Abingdon.
Probyn, E. (2005), *Blush: Faces of Shame*, Minneapolis: University of Minnesota Press.
Rabichev, R. (1996), 'The Mediterranean Concepts of Honour and Shame as Seen in the Depiction of the Biblical Women', *Religion and Theology*, 3(1), pp. 51–63.
Ramshaw, E. (1987), *Ritual and Pastoral Care*, Minneapolis: Fortress Press.
Raphael, M. (2003), *The Female Face of God in Auschwitz*, London: Routledge.
Reddie, A. G. (2019), *Theologising Brexit: a Liberationist and Postcolonial Critique*, Abingdon: Routledge.
Rogerson, J. (1991), *Genesis 1–11*, Sheffield: JSOT Press.
Rohrbaugh, R. L. (2010), 'Honor: Core Value in the Biblical World', in D. Neufeld and R. E. DeMaris, eds, *Understanding the Social World of the New Testament*, Abingdon: Routledge, pp. 109–25.
Ronson, J. (2015), *So You've Been Publicly Shamed*, London: Picador.
Rustomjee, S. (2009), 'The Solitude and Agony of Unbearable Shame', *Group Analysis* 42(2), pp. 143–55.
Sanderson, C. (2015), *Counselling Skills for Working with Shame*, London: Jessica Kingsley.
Sartain, D. and Katsarou, M. (2011), *Under Pressure: Understanding and Managing the Pressure and Stress of Work*, London: Marshall Cavendish Business.
Savage, S. (2007), 'Healing Encounters: Psychological Perspectives on Jesus' Healing', in F. Watts, ed., *Jesus and Psychology*, London: Darton, Longman and Todd, pp. 44–61.
Savage, T. B. (1996). *Power through Weakness: Paul's Understanding of the Christian Ministry in 2 Corinthians*, Cambridge: Cambridge University Press.
Sawyer, D. (1992), 'Resurrecting Eve?', in P. Morris and D. Sawyer, eds, *A Walk in the Garden: Biblical, Iconographical and Literary Images of Eden*, Sheffield: Sheffield Academic Press, pp. 273–89.

Sawyer, J. F. A. (1992), 'The Image of God, the Wisdom of Serpents and the Knowledge of Good and Evil', in P. Morris and D. Sawyer, eds, *A Walk in the Garden: Biblical, Iconographical and Literary Images of Eden*, Sheffield: Sheffield Academic Press, pp. 64–73.

Scheff, T. J. (1979), *Catharsis in Healing, Ritual and Drama*, Berkeley: University of California Press.

Scheff, T. J. (2011), 'Shame as the Master Emotion: Examples from Popular Songs', in R. Jewett, W. L. Alloway Jr. and J. G. Lacey, eds, *The Shame Factor: How Shame Shapes Society*, Eugene: Cascade Books, pp. 30–39.

Scheff, T. J., and Retzinger, S. M. (2001), *Emotions and Violence: Shame and Rage in Destructive Conflicts*, Lincoln, NE: iUniverse.

Schmader, T., and Lickel, B. (2006), 'The Approach and Avoidance Function of Guilt and Shame Emotions: Comparing Reactions to Self-caused and Other-caused Wrongdoing', *Motivation and Emotion*, 30(1), pp. 42–55.

Schneider, C. D. (1992), *Shame: Exposure and Privacy*, New York: Norton.

Schottroff, L. (1993), 'The Creation Narrative: Genesis 1.1–2.4a', in A. Brenner, ed., *A Feminist Companion to Genesis*, Sheffield: Sheffield Academic Press, pp. 24–38.

Sharman, J. (2018), 'What is the Billy Graham Rule?', *The Independent*, 21 February 2018, www.independent.co.uk/news/world/americas/billy-graham-rule-what-is-mike-pence-presidents-men-women-room-alone-dead-a8221416.html accessed 20 February 2019.

Shepherd, L., Spears, R. and Manstead, A. S. R. (2013), '"This Will Bring Shame on Our Nation": The Role of Anticipated Group-based Emotions on Collective Action', *Journal of Experimental Social Psychology*, 49(1), pp. 42–57.

Sieff, D. F., ed. (2015), *Understanding and Healing Emotional Trauma*, Hove: Routledge.

Smedes, L. B. (1993), *Shame and Grace: Healing the Shame We Don't Deserve*, San Francisco: HarperSanFrancisco.

Soneff, S. (2008), *Art Journals and Creative Healing*, Beverly: Quarry Books.

Stiebert, J. (2002), *The Construction of Shame in the Old Testament*, Sheffield: Sheffield University Press.

Stockitt, R. (2012), *Restoring the Shamed: Towards a Theology of Shame*, Eugene: Cascade Books.

Streaty Wimberly, A. E. (2011), 'Overcoming Shame in Slave Songs and the Epistle to the Hebrews', in R. Jewett, W. L. Alloway Jr. and J. G. Lacey, eds, *The Shame Factor: How Shame Shapes Society*, Eugene: Cascade Books, pp. 60–85.

Swinton, J. (2000), *Resurrecting the Person*, Nashville: Abingdon Press.

Swinton, J., and Mowat, H. (2006), *Practical Theology and Qualitative Research*, London: SCM Press.

Tangney, J. P. and Dearing, R. L. (2002), *Shame and Guilt*, New York: The Guilford Press.

Tennent, T. C. (2007), *Theology in the Context of World Christianity*, Grand Rapids: Zondervan.

Thiselton, A. C. (1980), *The Two Horizons: New Testament Hermeneutics and Philosophical Description with Special Reference to Heidegger, Bultmann, Gadamer and Wittgenstein*, Exeter: Paternoster.

Thiselton, A. C. (1992), *New Horizons in Hermeneutics*, London: Marshall Pickering.

Thiselton, A. C. (2000), *The First Epistle to the Corinthians: The New International Greek Testament Commentary*, Carlisle: Paternoster.

Tillman-Samuelson, D. J. (2018), 'Women Leaders in Christian Higher Education: Resilience in Moments of Shame', unpublished PhD thesis, Gonzaga University.

Thomas, R., and Parker, S. (2004), 'Towards a Theological Understanding of Shame', *Journal of Psychology and Christianity*, 23(2), pp. 176–82.

Thompson, C. (2015), *The Soul of Shame: Retelling the Stories We Believe about Ourselves*, Downers Grove, IL: InterVarsity Press.

Thompson, K. (2011), *Therapeutic Journal Writing*, London: Jessica Kingsley.

Towner, W. S. (2001), *Genesis*, Louisville: Westminster John Knox.

van Eck, E. (2011), 'When Neighbours Are Not Neighbours: A Social-scientific Reading of the Parable of the Friend at Midnight (Lk. 11.5–8)', *HTS Teologiese Studies/Theological Studies*, 67(1), pp. 1–14.

Ward, P. (2017), *Introducing Practical Theology*, Grand Rapids: Baker Academic.

Watson, D. F. (2010), *Honor Among Christians*, Minneapolis: Fortress Press.

Watson, J. (2005), *Shame*, Cambridge: Grove P101.

Wells, S. (2013), *Learning to Dream Again: Rediscovering the Heart of God*, Norwich: Canterbury Press.

Whitehead, E. E. and Whitehead, J. D. (2003), *Shadows of the Heart A Spirituality of Painful Emotions*, Lincoln, NE: Authors Guild.

Wilder, W. N. (2006), 'Illumination and Investiture: The Royal Significance of the Tree of Wisdom in Genesis 3', *Westminster Theological Journal*, 68(1), pp. 51–69.

Williams, R. H. (2010), 'Purity, Dirt, Anomalies, and Abominations', in D. Neufeld and R. E. DeMaris, eds, *Understanding the Social World of the New Testament*, Abingdon: Routledge, pp. 207–19.

Wimberly, E. P. (1999), *Moving from Shame to Self-Worth*, Nashville, TN: Abingdon Press.

Wimberly, E. P. (2011), *No Shame in Wesley's Gospel: A Twenty-First Century Pastoral Theology*, Eugene, OR: Wipf and Stock.

Witherington, B. III (1995), *Conflict and Community in Corinth: A Socio-Rhetorical Commentary on 1 and 2 Corinthians*, Grand Rapids: Eerdmans.

Woien, S. L., Ernst, H. A. H., Patock-Peckham, J. A. and Nagoshi, C. T. (2003), 'Validation of the TOSCA to Measure Shame and Guilt', *Personality and Individual Differences*, 35(2), pp. 313–26.

Womersley, G., Maw, A. & Swartz, S. (2011), 'The Construction of Shame in Feminist Reflexive Practice and Its Manifestations in a Research Relationship', *Qualitative Inquiry*, 17, pp. 876–86.

Wright, A. W. (2008), 'The Power of Testimonies', in M. E. Moore and A. W. Wright, eds, *Children, Youth and Spirituality in a Troubling World*, St Louis, MO: Chalice Press, pp. 182–95.

Wurmser, L. (1997), *The Mask of Shame*, Northvale: Jason Aronson.

Yee, G. A. (2003), *Poor Banished Children of Eve*, Minneapolis: Fortress Press.

Young, R. (1898), *Young's Literal Translation of the Holy Bible*, Grand Rapids: Baker Book House.

Index of Bible References

Index of Names and Subjects